More Critical Praise

"If you don't know the na
—*The Stranger*

"Nicole Blackman speaks to us in a compassionate voice which under-
stands the tiny bruises and life-threatening disasters which plague our
day-to-day existence. Blood Sugar is salve to the wounds, self-inflicted or
not, which we all have a desperate need to heal." —Lydia Lunch

"Blackman anatomizes the experience of today's girl . . . the sound of
thoughts processing at many megahertz inside her head." —*Artforum*

"Compelling, psychosexual lyric forays." —*Billboard*

"Incisive . . . as chilling as it is real. Sure to make the hairs on the back
of your neck stand ever-so-slightly on end. She gives voice to the dead,
missing, forgotten and condemned." —*Time Out New York*

"Sweet talk, poison tongue. She's not making history, she's just breaking it
up into rhythmic syllables and watching us swallow piece by prickly piece
. . . Although Blackman whispers and coos in the ear of her audience,
some of her lines speak enough to shatter glass houses." —*Resonance*

"She's kind of like the Judy Blume for grownup outcasts, offering solace
where Gap ads don't." —*Outburn*

"Spoken word has produced a few international stars, such as Nicole
Blackman . . . [Her] words are sexy, stylish, and subtle, yet have all the
force of a semi-trailer." —PBS FM/Australia

"Emma Peel . . . could never shoot bullets as straight as Nicole does
words. No pretentious frills; just one thought-provoking statement after
another. Miss Blackman gets it right." —*Flipside*

"A very pretty hate machine." —*Pandemonium*

"She's erotic, icy and accusatory—Laurie Anderson working a 1-900 line."
—*CMJ Monthly*

BLOOD SUGAR
NICOLE BLACKMAN

Akashic Books
New York

ISBN 1-888451-34-3
Second Akashic Books printing

Printed in Canada

Art direction and book design by Gary Hustwit
Cover and author photos by Jimmy Cohrssen

Poems in this collection previously appeared in the author's chapbooks *Pretty, Sweet,* and *Nice* (Spy Verses Spy), in the anthologies *Aloud: Voices from the Nuyorican Poets Cafe* (W.W. Norton), *Verses That Hurt: Pleasure and Pain from the Poemfone Poets* (St. Martin's), *Revival: Spoken Word from Lollapalooza '94* (Manic D Press), *Poetry Nation* (Vehicule), *Will Work For Peace: New Political Poems* (Zeropanik), in the photo book *Twilight* with Jimmy Cohrssen, in the magazines *New York Quarterly, Bust, Gargoyle, Cups, Excursus, Elle Singapore, Tribe, Barrow Street, Cordite, Flexible Head, Oculus, Carbon 14,* and *The Fuse*; on the recordings Golden Palominos *Dead Inside* (Restless), KMFDM *Xtort* (Wax Trax!/TVT), Recoil *Liquid* (Mute), *Teleconned: We Want The Airwaves - Vol. 1* (No Alternative), *Poemfone: New Word Order* (Tomato), *Myth: Dreams of the World* (Dove Audio), *Indie Rock Blueprint* (Go! Discs), *Images of My Underworld, Vol. III* (Horrorshow), *Family* (Tongue'n'groove), and the author's *Indictment/I Believe* 7" (Carcrashh).

Thank you: Alex Beard, Sean Beavan, Caeri Bertrand, Mark Blasquez, Delphine Blue + WBAI, Carrie Borzillo, Juliette Bradley, Gwendolyn Brooks, Scott Byron, Regie Cabico, Lori Carson, Betty Cobb, Jimmy Cohrssen, Mandy Cox + ARD, Katie Deatrick, Marnie Dunstan, Brian Duong + The Cool Kids of Death, Lawrence English, Jessicka, Anton Fier, Karen Finley, Diamanda Galas, Joseph Garland, Maria Ferrero, Sohrab Habibion, Glen Hirshberg + Campbell Hall, Gary Hustwit, The ICM Agency, Johanna Ingalls, Casey Kait, Paul Kendall, Jim Kenefick + The French Underground, KMFDM, Bill Laswell, Anna Kim, Irene Lavina, Lydia Lunch, Glenn Max + Knitting Factory, Colin McComb, Willy McLachlan, Chris Morgan, the Nuyorican Poets Cafe, Siobhan O'Neill, William Packard, Richard Peabody, Jason Pettigrew, Liza Richardson + KCRW, Janet Rienstra, Robin Rimbaud, Hepzibah Sessa, Shawn Stewart + REV 105, Todd Swift, Johnny Temple, Jordy + Amy Trachtenberg, Harry Volk Jr., Raymond Watts, Alan + Paris Wilder, Lauren Zelisko, and anyone who didn't know I was listening and taking notes.

http://www.nicole-blackman.com

Akashic Books
PO Box 1456
New York, NY 10009
Akashic7@aol.com
www.akashicbooks.com

CONTENTS

to my sun and moon

Jeannemarie Volk McGowan
and John Van Eaton

I am writing with my burnt hand about
the nature of fire. –Ingeborg Bachmann

I'm going to show you something very ugly.
One day it may save your life. –W.D. Snodgrass

GIRLS

When he leaves,
he leaves a space,
a big or little airless place
that begs to be filled.
A part of the weekend that says
What are you going to do now?

And you think if you fill it up
you'll survive.
So you work and clean and call
and cook and write and drink
and read and sleep and shop
and say *This is fine this is fine.*
You can do this.

Laugh and go out drinking
with your friends when it's over.
Call everyone you know and say
whatever.
Shrug, clear your throat.

It's kind of like losing a dog.
You'll miss him
but maybe it's better this way.

His friends are still your friends
sometimes
and they watch you
because they send him messages
about how you're doing.
Sometimes they figure now is their chance
and they tell you they've always had it bad
for you.

Be careful with his friends.

So cut your hair
and learn to play guitar.
Walk fast and yell back
at bike messengers who tell you
what they'd do to you
if you were theirs.

Stop wearing his coat and sell his CDs.
White out his name in your address book.
Buy new perfume and learn to masturbate
with the showerhead.
Turn the pain into something you can use.

And when it feels like you're imploding,
like you're the only one
who wants to lie down in the street,
know that there will always be girls
who stream through this city
with their mouths slightly open
trying to breathe
and waiting to be kissed.

KIM

Kim's getting off the heroin
and she shows me her cold ivory arms in a diner later
as if it's evidence to an uncaring judge.

She peels her nails down in front of me,
layer by layer, like a paper onion.

She's started smoking again,
has slept with her landlord,
claims she wants to leave New York.

What makes her think she can start over again anywhere in this world
and not have it be exactly the same?

She pours salt into her coffee by accident
— drinks it anyway.

She tells the cashier to keep the change
because she likes to travel light.

Later she'll scream to me from the corner because she has no quarters
to make a phone call.

When we say goodbye, I can see her,
moving so slowly through air
like a feather that cannot fight on its way down.

BROOKLYN

and you ask *is this okay?*
is this okay?
and I sweep soft hands
around your shoulders
dragging you slowly to me
while you use little words
like *pretty*

and you fear I will feel less
that this will be less fine than before
and what you do, you do
and undo me

and I sink into white pillows
and feel you unfold against me
with moonbeams beating
noiselessly at the window

and heaven is caught between us
like a wish too uncool to speak

and this one is a mistake
and this one is a memory

and afterwards you ask how I am
and I use words like *perfect*
and wonder if I mean them

and I lie here
knowing that
somewhere there's another girl
lying in another cold room
listening to the sound
of her breath

and later I'll scour your room for clues
(while you're out getting orange juice)
and will spend my days
hoping you're thinking
I'm a girl worth keeping

and I don't care what you are
because I'll make you
into whatever I need,
and will stroke you to sleep
while I murmur and burn

SESSIONS

I am part of a small story
in a big house
a damaged messenger
who lost her credibility.

It's not easy to turn him in, you know.
They'll tell you you're dreaming
lying fibbing fantasizing.
If I was going to fantasize
it wouldn't be about this, ma'am.

You are my child psychologist
so I tell you everything
in words measured as carefully
as sugar.
Then you tell me to tell you again
and I tell you.
And I beg.

And you tell me to tell you again.
Trying to trip me up.
You're not on my side, are you?

So you bundle me up
and return me to hell
and wonder why I don't want
to talk to you next Tuesday.
I think this part is worse
than what he did to me.
All of this is terror
and all of this is night.

I've paid my way at an early age
and have seen my silhouette
cause wars in houses.
I stumble around like a nightmare reported.

I'm not growing up, just evolving.
I'm only eleven and people shut their doors
when I walk by.

DAUGHTER

One day I'll give birth to a tiny baby girl
and when she's born she'll scream
and I'll tell her to never stop.

I will kiss her before I lay her down at night
and will tell her a story so she knows
how it is and how it must be for her to survive.

I'll tell her to set things on fire
and keep them burning.
I'll teach her that fire will not consume her,
that she must use it.

I'll tell her that people must earn the right
to use her nickname,
that forced intimacy is an ugly thing.

I'll help her to see that she will not find God
or salvation in a dark brick building
built by dead men.

I'll make sure she always carries a pen
so she can take down the evidence.
If she has no paper, I'll teach her to
write everything down with her tongue,
write it on her thighs.

I'll make her keep reinventing herself and run fast.
I'll teach her to write her manifestos
on cocktail napkins.
I'll say she should make men lick her ambition.
I'll make her understand that she is worth more
with her clothes on.
I'll teach her to talk hard.

I'll tell her that when the words come too fast
and she has no use for a pen
that she must quit her job
run out of the house in her bathrobe,
leave the door open.
I'll teach her to follow the words.

They will try to make her stay,
comfort her, let her sleep, bathe her in a television blue glow.
I will cut her hair, tell her to light the house on fire,
kill the kittens,
when nothing is there
nothing will keep her
and she is not to be kept.

I'll say that everything she has done seen spoken
has brought her to the here this now.
This is no time for tenderness,
no time to stand, waiting for them to find her.
There are nations within her skin.
Queendoms come without keys you can carry.

I'll teach her that she has an army inside her
that can save her life.
I'll teach her to be whole, to be holy.
I'll teach her how to live,
to be so much that she doesn't even
need me anymore.
I'll tell her to go quickly and never come back.
Things get broken fast here.

I will make her stronger than I ever was.

Turned at twenty
she'll break into bits of star
and throw herself against the sky.

(1999 is an excellent year
to disappear)

I will not let them destroy her life
the way they destroyed mine.

I'll tell her to never forget what they did to you
and never let them know you remember.

Never forget what they did to you
and never let them know you remember.

Never forget what they did to you
and never let them know you remember.

CHRISTIAN'S CALLING

Christian is just learning to speak.
He unravels over the phone like a sweater.

He's loyal to the wrong friend
he's in love with the wrong girl
he's destroyed by the rest of the world.

Christian keeps a box under his bed.
He whispers in his sleep.
He always carries his passport with him
in case he has to suddenly disappear.
It's taken him a year to trust me.

Sometimes when he thinks
no one's looking
he touches the scars on his throat
where she nearly clawed him to death.

I parked outside her house today,
he says. *I didn't go in. I didn't
want her to see me. I didn't know
what I wanted, but this hurts,*
he says. *It hurts out loud. I can
hold it in my hands and it's so
heavy,* he cries, *it's just so heavy.*

Christian boils down his days to
coffee, errands, bills, regrets,
daydreams, drinks, crying fits,
phone calls, nightmares.

One night he falls
onto a strange new blanket of skin.
He tells me later that things are better.

Don't worry about me, he says,
I'm getting it somewhere else now.

In two days he's brittle again,
a china boy who chips away at his skin
just to see how little it takes to leave a mark.

Was it like this before? he asks.
Will it be like this forever?
I can't choke out a yes.
Long distance is too far away
to risk a suicide.
On his way to a date with some
interim girl, he gets a message on
his pager. She cancels his chance,
ending his night before it's begun.
He calls me from a payphone,
halfway across the world, and says
I'm all messed up with no place to
go.

(The lions pick their teeth
clean with your bones.
Christian, your only crime
is that you fell in love with a lion.)

I hear the catch in his voice and
he breaks down, tearing apart like silk.
I just don't want to go home.
I just don't want to go home alone,
he whispers, as if the oxygen
costs too much. If only I
could reach across the country
to the dark parking lot
where he's falling apart a piece
at a time.

(The lions smell your blood
and breathe in your dust.
If they destroy you, Christian
it's because they must.)

And the little god
with the broken head
and the broken heart
sighs and beats the time.

I have come to Los Angeles to die,
he moans.
I have come to Los Angeles to die.

LOST

I've lost my notebook.
I've lost a poem.

It was a great one.
It was eleven pages long.

It was about my father saying he couldn't hear me.
It was about the *X* I cut into the back of my hand.

It was about seeing yet another friend on heroin.
It was about that little boy kicking a bird to death.

It was about the four leaf clover someone sent me.
It was about the time I could not stop sleeping.

It was about mailing anonymous hate letters.
It was about finding bruises all over my legs.

It was about the bartender who wouldn't let me pay.
It was about trying to find the cool spot on the pillow.

It was about the lipstick I stole from a girl's medicine cabinet.
It was about seeing my favorite poet shake when she gave a reading.

It was about the tape I ripped out of someone's answering machine.
It was about the friend who banged on my door and I did not let her in.

It was about watching MTV after school and wondering
        if I'd look like that when I grew up.
It was about my mother lying on the kitchen floor
        and the dog licking her face.

It was about what happened when I forgot how much milk
    my boyfriend liked in his coffee.
It was about the time I read someone's diary
    and ripped out the pages about me.

It was about going to the bus station and not knowing where I was going.
It was about coming in late for a movie and kissing through the credits.

It was about the car I could not drive.
It was about my party when no one came.

It was about the last time you touched me.
It was about the way you walked away.

It was the best thing I'd ever written.
It was everything I wanted to say.

I've lost my notebook.
I've lost a poem.

THIRST
(for John)

Your mouth as necessary on mine as rain on the desert
(I remember thirst).
I remember unloading guns beneath a complex heaven
(they cut into my dreams).
I remember how bitterness tasted
(it was sometimes sweet).

Now in the black black behind your sleep
I am trying to hold your oceans
I am struggling to sparkle in your sky
I will collect your snowfalls in my arms
and watch them unfold.

●   ●   ●

In the North, you ache with loss
and wish for a sick day
to curl yourself away and cry.
The warmth of your voice
now burnt with loss
and everyone knows.

Everyone knows you are far too far
too transparent
to hide away such a wanting.
Now whom is needed
and whom is needful?

You are older than I
but hand your small self over
— a bird nestling into my hand.
I am broken, I am broken
you say as I stroke you to sleep.

Making the day's tea of desperation
I know you are sterling.
No, I won't tell them.
No, I won't share you.
I am killing myself trying not to care.

•   •   •

I know you're too fine for this.
They've raised your hopes
now they've come to dash them.
Let me throw you deep into the stars
so you can see your heaven
and speak to your dead.

(Lay on me the hands that never kill.
Stain my skin with breath
laced in coolth and stun.
Trace my form in the dark until it glows.)

You are younger than your years
and I am older than mine.
Some midnight I will meet you in the midst
and cross your palm with my mouth.

•   •   •

Come here little bird
let me lick your feathers back.
Come here to your complicated cat.

I have done my best to steer you away
now I swim in blame and sleep in fear.
When we go public, my china bird
I'll let you tell the story.

When you hurt me
I won't let it show.

DROWN

I am sick with this

his scent swims around me
like a perfume too heavy for summer
me, lost thing
intoxicated
curled within him
drowning over and over

charmed disarmed
he comes when least expected
sits too close
lingers too long
stares too deeply
and claims me with something I cannot name

lightheaded and clean
this is a gift
biting tongue until blood
I am sick with him

talk goes no deeper than tonight
words are tickets to spend time
skin is talking to skin
loud

I know not to go too deep
but when his hands stop
tremble, temptation
I thrill back
open up
crawl walls

this woman is no man's
this man is no one's
this one is mine

•

smitten
it vibrates
makes drinks tremble
food wastes time
cigarettes are for curling smoke
and drawing me in

this is bloody business

guilt makes for poor postcards
so he comes in for a while
what do we know of this?

doesn't know if he'll be allowed to stay
but he looks a while too long
and stirs the close air
dragging me to the bottom of the lake

couches are for excuses
and temptation
crushed in too deep to breathe
swoon against skin you do not know
with hands that know too much
of what you must never say

flesh to curl to grind
to feign sleep to balance wishes
on tongues and wait for the time
now

cozy he calls me
says I smell like sweet cream

closed eyes bring on a luscious film
of time and silence

he tastes like stars
he feels like thunder

regret makes you bitter
he says
come in and swim

we disappear into a dusk
we'll never own
and never quite shake

a luscious slice
of water
lack of sleep makes me drift
lake of sleep makes me wonder

●

he will exist
he will evaporate
I am sick with him gone

in regret dreams he is low and sweet
dark like a drift storm
holding me down under the waves
telling me not to talk
not to move
this will only take an hour
or two

HOLY

I eat only sleep and air
and everyone thinks I'm dumb
but I'm smart because I've figured it out.

I am slimmer than you are
and I am burning my skin off little by little
until I reach bone and self
until I get to where I am essential
until I get to where I am.

Food doesn't tempt me anymore
because I am so full of energy and sense
I can even pass by water now
because I am living off the parts of me
that I don't need anymore.

I could feel the slow drips of pain before
swirling inside where my lungs should have been.
Now I'm clean inside.

I threw out hundreds of things that I didn't need anymore.
All my dresses and bras
stupid things like jeans and socks.
Most days I float through the house naked
so I can see myself in the mirrors.
I have hundreds of them everywhere
and they talk back to me all the time.
They keep me true and pure.
They make sure I'm still here.

When I knew what I had to do
I took all my notebooks, all my manuscripts
and ate them page by page
so I could take my words with me.

I can finally control my life
and even death
and I will die slowly like steam escaping from a pipe.

This is my greatest performance
and all of the actresses who won my parts will say
how wonderful to let yourself go that mad
how wonderful to go on this kind of journey
and not care if you come back to tell the story.

I scratch words on the walls now
so people will visit this museum and know
how someone like me ends up like this
(they'll say there is art in here somewhere).

Everything that comes out of me is sacred
every tear, every cough, every piss.
Everything that comes off of me is sacred
every fingernail, every eyelash, every hair.

Starvation is sacred and I scratch my bones
against the windows at night.
I light candles and feel myself evaporate.
This body is a little church, a little temple.
You can't see me now because I've gone inside.

My family doesn't call anymore.
My friends don't call anymore.
You can't hurt me anymore.
They can't hurt me anymore.
Only I can.

And that's okay.
I don't need them anymore.
I can live off of me.
I speak to me.
I dance with me.
I eat me.

When they find me, I'll have a little smile on my face
and they'll wrap me in a white cloth and lay me in the ground
and say they don't understand.
But I do.
I don't hurt anymore.
I'm not lonely anymore.
I'm not sad I'm not pretty anymore.
I made it through.

I feel so holy and clean when I stretch out on the floor and sing.
Sometimes god comes in for a minute and says I'm doing fine
I'm almost there.

Every day I get a little closer to vanishing.
Some days I can't stand up because the room moves under my feet
and I smile because I'm almost there
I'm almost an angel.

One day when I am thin enough
I'll go outside
fluttering my hands so I can fly
and I will be so slight that I will pass through all of you
silently
like wind.

TO JULIAN (WHO IS NOT JULIAN, BUT THAT IS ENOUGH)

He does not notice her
but she cannot stop noticing him,
feeling his heat as he passes behind her,
even on the other side of the room.
He drinks and talks and smokes and pays
no mind to lighting her cigarette.
She waits and lights it herself.
Shunned.

When he is deep in thought and perfume
she goes into the bathroom and in the bare light
rubs her wrists where she wishes he'd kiss her
(and give her the choice).

She is forgettable because she is nearly a boy.
She is forgettable because she is always there when he calls.
She is forgettable because she chides him,
hoping one day she'll say something harsh enough so he'll hit her
so at least he'll touch her then,
so she can break through and forgive him his invisible trespasses,
as if this is about grace,
as if that is enough.

He does not photograph her
but he photographs all his other women,
the conquests with the single names and funny stories.
She hears about them all and laughs with him
over oceans of vodka.

She does not ask
but when he sees her looking at the photographs
he says *I could never photograph you,*
I could never capture your beauty

and grins so she knows he's lying.
He can't do her portrait until he's cracked her open.
Silently, she knows this is about more than fear.
It is about terror and the terror is his.

When he is wrapped around another woman's skinny bones,
she quietly breaks into his darkroom next door
and stands beneath his wall of black and red women
and takes out her x-acto blade.

When she hears him cry out
she cuts out their eyes
one by one.

GONE

When I am gone your pillows will smell like me.

When I am gone the ice cubes in your glass and
the sway of your curtains will sound like me.

When I am gone your toothbrush and milk carton will taste like me.

When I am gone everyone who passes by your window
and everyone on your television will look like me.

When I am gone the curve of your telephone,
the blade of your razor,
and the fur of your cat will feel like me.

When I am gone you will tell your landlady
that you're leaving at the end of the month.

You will swear your apartment is haunted.

MISSING NATALIE

Most of my friends don't know I was born a twin. She was born sixty-three seconds before me. Her name was Natalie. We came here together. She left without me.

We shared a room and split it down the middle. I put all my posters up on my side, and she put hers up on the other. One day we decided to wallpaper the room with Superfriends wrapping paper and Elmer's glue. Mom wasn't too crazy about that.

She was patient, I was bossy. She wanted to be a gymnast, I wanted to be an actress. But we both liked horses and we liked to draw. We mixed up things like ketchup and cough syrup and tried to get someone to eat it. Natalie and I would climb trees in our backyard and plan the houses we would build next to each other so we could visit when we had families of our own. We picked out the names for our husbands, for our children. When you're a twin, you have a shadow.

We were in the supermarket looking at the toys. Mom was picking up some shampoo and cat food. There was a doll that I really wanted so I ran a couple aisles over to ask Mom. She told me I already had too many dolls and sent me back to get Natalie so we could leave the store. It all happened in a minute.

This is the part where I'm supposed to tell you that your life can change forever in sixty-three seconds. But you already know that, don't you?

On the surveillance camera, you can see Natalie walking out of the store with a man. He's not forcing her, but we don't know why she's going with him. She turns around for a second like she's saying goodbye. At least that's what we think it means.

We've gone over the video hundreds of times. It's burned in my mind like the Zapruder film. Even now I could draw it for you, with the time code on the bottom of the screen and everything.

I'm twenty-four now. She's frozen at nine.

When she was gone a month, I put our beds together and put a blanket across them when I slept.

They sent me to a child psychologist for a long time. She made me draw my "feelings." *Let's draw your feelings now. What do your feelings look like?* I wanted to strangle her. Instead, I drew for an hour so she'd shut up. I used only the black markers and drew me and a burned-out hole for Natalie. *That's me, and that's Natalie.* The psychologist analyzed the drawings and talked to my parents. *She's having a very difficult time. Losing Natalie has left a void in her life.* Well, duh. You could have just asked me and saved yourself a lot of time. *You want to know how I feel? You want to know what's going on? Someone stole my sister. Someone fucking stole my sister. How many drawings do you want me to make?* They stopped making me go to the psychologist after that.

I never saw Dad cry but something was sacrificed after it happened. He drinks alone now sometimes. He never used to do that.

The police give us a report every three years now or something, and tell us the case is still open, as if that's a help. They try to tell me sometimes that since they never found a body, she might be alive. Right. Like there's nowhere on earth to hide a body. If she was alive, I'd know. If anyone would know I'd know and I haven't felt her near me in a long, long time.

They put me under hypnosis. I told them the man was wearing a navy blue corduroy jacket, had brown work boots on, smelled of grease and never looked at me. The case is still open.

Four months after she disappeared, it was our tenth birthday. I told Mom to forget about it but she insisted...she always had a birthday party for us...we had to go on with a normal life. The day of the party we hung up balloons and streamers and Mom pretended Natalie was away somewhere, like it was a surprise. I sat there and waited. I waited all day.

Nobody came. All the kids who used to come to our parties now said they couldn't. Sometimes their mothers called and cancelled, like abductions were contagious and they didn't want their kids to catch it too.

That night Mom and I sat in the kitchen and ate a box of sugar cookies and talked about Natalie. We didn't have anymore birthday parties after that. It became the birthday ritual. We would eat a whole box of sugar cookies and talk about Natalie for hours. It was our way of keeping her close. We do it every year. Dad still doesn't know.

My parents refused to move after Natalie disappeared. *We need to be here when she comes back. Otherwise, how will she find us?*

We just want to know what happened. It's like watching a scary movie and the film breaks in the last fifteen minutes and they try to make everyone go home. We just want to know what happened.

Most of my friends don't even know I was born a twin. She was born sixty-three seconds before me. Her name was Natalie. We came here together. She left without me.

TO THE BOY WHO EXPLODED
TO THE BOY WHO DROWNED
TO THE BOY WHO FELL FROM STARS

dead to me now, all dead to me
dying again and again with each telling
you agony kings
you you you false martyrs
who ran for the door
just before the check came.

damn the timing
and bless it too
america loves her sons who die
before their turn to cash in
stay dead, you're beautiful there
(that's where we love you best).

there is some gory ballet in the way
we tell the details of the crash
the car, the party, the necklace.
there is some physical release
at the punchline:
only half a mile from home.
just signed the record deal.
body so far gone he was identified
only by the padlock around his neck.
we take something from the site
every time we speak of it. some shell
some piece of twisted metal to slip in
our pocket, some clue that might be
crucial to the police but we take it anyway
(like vultures, like rats).
this private grief hung in public
as if it proves something about us
how much we knew of his life
how close we must have been to him
(closer than you, motherfucker, closer than you).

•   •   •

walking into the river
with your heavy boots on.
how dumb.
but everyone forgives a beautiful boy
and your black baptism held you undertow
under cool wet sheets
that pulled you down and down
for days until you rose
bloated and blue
and your mother said
I didn't think my son would ever walk out of the river...
and the internet girls wrung their hands
and said *woe woe*
while dj's at stations that never played your songs
played entire album sides in tribute
to a famous dead boy
with a famous dead father.
did you swallow water, did you swallow blood?
(thursday I watched your soundscan fly).

•   •   •

easy to touch stars when they glow in the dark
on your bedroom ceiling, the green a sickening cast.
you could count stars but you couldn't capture them.
you could name them but you couldn't keep them.
who would let you have them?
when you flew under them you could not taste them in the cold.
after years of being on the wrong side of the sky
you crept up at night and offered yourself from a rooftop and
reached up
jumped into the night's lace expecting some bright god
impressed
to lift you out of the twisted air into the dark dark blue.

they say the suicide usually dies of a heart attack
before he ever reaches ground
that there is a moment of redemption in mid-air
that the jumper waves and shakes his body trying to stop
stop
stop
did you see stars when you landed?
were you burning when you fell?

•   •   •

did all of you know the moment God took you back?
did you say a prayer or curse the dark?
did you relax and surrender or struggle against
the explosion the water the earth?
(the ground now soft for lack of your steps)

and do you have any words for us
the ones who clean out storage rooms and sell guitars
the ones who make statements to the press
and tell everyone we're doing fine now
and please make a donation in your name?

THE BAD SHEPARD
(for Matthew Shepard)

Someone beat that boy a while. Someone burned that boy alive. Dear dead boy did they tell you the truth? Did they lie about the cost? Is it your blood they wear now? Do they sleep like babies, do they sleep like storms? Will they ever sleep again like you do now? Dear dead boy are you sleeping softly now?

Someone beat that boy a while. Someone burned that boy alive. You must have been so scared. Did they tell you what they'd do to you before they did it? Did Jesus and Joan stand by you and guide you through? Saying "they killed us the way they're killing you." How strong were you before they broke you? Was it for this that you were born?

Someone beat that boy a while. Someone burned that boy alive. Did the undertaker sew up what was left of your mouth? Did he sew up what was left of your eyes? Did your mother recognize you in the casket? Did she say "that's what he looked like when he slept?" Did she say "did they know what they were taking away when they took away my boy?"

Our father, who art in heaven, hollow be thy name. In the book of love, was there no page for you? Did you know how to suffer? Did you think you'd survive? They were feeling enraged they were feeling entitled. We are not brothers, we are not the same. The terrible things done in God's name.

Our father, who art in heaven, hollow be thy name. As a boy you mistook angels for aliens and thought heaven was strung with a lace of lights. A soft hunter, now hunted. A slight boy, slighted.

Our father, who art in heaven, hollow be thy name. On a dark night in a wide field you begged "so help me, God...so help me, God" and waited in vain for a response. You believed that God loved all his children. That night did you think God loved you less? That God loved you a little bit less?

One of these boys was not like the others. One of these boys was not quite the same. When you were a young boy they boxed your ears and put you down. When you were a young man they boxed you up and put you in the ground. Now you are hung in clouds and we think we can see you.

One of these boys was not like the others. One of these boys was not quite the same. The world would like to know what happened. The world would like you to know how sorry they are. They cut you so deep, they went to the bone. When they were done killing you, they went home.

The terrible things done in God's name. Heaven will not hold all of you now.

One of these boys was not like the others. One of these boys was not quite the same. Now your name is written in roses.

Someone beat that boy a while. Someone burned that boy alive. Now your name is written in roses. Someone will burn them too.

This is how we kill our boys in Laramie.
This is how we kill our boys in Wyoming.
This is how we kill our boys in America.
This is how we kill our boys.

This is how we kill our boys.

IN THE MOVIE NOW

There is no glory in trying to make love to men
who only know how to fuck —
man after man after man after man
raised on porn.

Out all day while he's been watching $2 videos
now piled by the VCR,
out all day at work at class at the gym
while he's making plans
out all day returning with bags of bread
and tomatoes and bluefish for what you think
will be dinner.

Dinner is you
and you are nothing like
the dead-eyed blonde women
he's been watching.

You're in the movie now.

He is nothing like you remember.
No time for a condom, take a pill
or put in a diaphragm.
Those girls never get pregnant anyway.
What are you trying to do?

Clothes cannot come off fast enough
get them off get them off
shoes are always left on
you don't know why.
You're in the movie now.

You used to scrape your nails
against the walls leaving

streaks like scars of where
you wanted to stay
and where he took you.

Now you just go
it'll be over
in ten minutes
it'll be over
in ten minutes
twenty at most.

A black envelope closes with you inside.
You're in the movie now.

He winds your hair around his fist
like a roll and he keeps it nailed to the bed.
You swear you'll cut your hair tomorrow.
You swear you'll cut your hair tomorrow.

You still swim in memory sometimes.
It wasn't always like this, was it?

You are becoming stone
stone desires nothing
stone cannot be moved
stone can only be worn down
little by little.

Close your eyes and think of England.

You are tucked in for the fucking.
You're in the movie now.

There is no beauty in being held face down
on a bed of sheets that tear beneath you
and you are wearing him like a country

you haven't the strength to carry.
You're in the movie now.

You don't fight
he takes it from you
he takes it from you
he takes it from you.
Now it isn't yours, how could it be?
Isn't yours anymore, never will be again.

One eye open, focusing on a window.
Years of this
and you don't even say anything anymore.
This is how it is
how it will always be.
You're in the movie now.

Cosmo has not told you what to do
in these circumstances.
Mademoiselle has not advised you
of snappy one-liners to use.
Ms. has not written an empowering column about this one.

It doesn't hurt anymore you shut down examining fibers in the pillow-
case counting them until he's finished 77-78-79 he says *look at me look
at me it's no good unless you look at me* you look right through him look
at your bookshelf your grandmother's patio your list of things to do this
weekend the basil leaves drying by the window.

He says if you cry it makes him angry.
I fuck better when I'm angry you know.
You know.
He says it every time.
You learn not to cry.

You are startled that he is doing this to you.

You are startled that he knows how.
You are startled that you stay
knowing you would tell a friend to kill him
if he did this to her.

Your mouth is on fire with possibilities.
You say nothing.

You shut down your body one limb at a time
like you learned in drama class relaxation exercises.
Absence of pain makes anything possible.

You used to confuse this with caring
you used to confuse these with caresses.
Desire doesn't live here anymore
desire doesn't live here anymore.

Because you are pretty you are possessed.
You two are alone, owner and owned.

You are turned over and over
backstrokes in your own blood
(horses have been christened with less).

There is no glory here
only bloodstains
and apologies that come with the stroking,
only throwing up in a sink
you'll have to scrub out later.

THE GOD OF SLEEP

Feel how skin goes sick in want of warmth
C'mon he says *come closer to me.*
He says your fingertips are blackened
like a gingerman cookie left in too long.
Girl, were you singed? Did someone burn you?

the god of warning and distance
the god of *I'm under instructions to do this*

He's seen you without your face
and he know how you feel inside.
It could have been sex with the perfect stranger
but he is neither.

the god of bracelets and necklaces
the god of ice and knives
the god of *I can turn you over on the floor in a minute*
the god of *I will turn on you*

He says he just wants to take a picture of you, pretty in his bed.
When he turns his back, rip the film out of the camera.

the god of razors and moon rivers
the god of dares and *surely you've done this before*
the god of answering machines
the god of *you bruise easily for a hard girl*

Here is your crucible, your severe test.
Here you are a crucible,
heat-resistant, used for melting things down.
You used to ask *can I sleep here?*
Now you know you can, but you don't dare.

the god of ashtrays and ashes
the god of *why did you turn your back to me?*
the god of soft hands and grinding teeth
the god of *was that a genuine sign of tenderness?*
the god of burns and scratches

In shadow and sheets you wonder
why all men look like princes when they sleep.
You won't be able to wash his scent off your skin for days.

the god of sleep and sleeplessness
the god of curved silver rings
the god of tea and tinnitis
the god of guilt

The next morning, smile and whisper
It was purely sport. I was just having fun.
Stand up as you button your shirt and say
You can't break my heart. I haven't got one.

the god of *we'll keep this just between us*

Don't you dare stick around for breakfast.
Out on the street, find a shadow quickly
so you can collapse and no one will see.

the god of *I'm rather embarrassed about the other night*
the god of fever pitch, yawn and chasm

It's easy to spot you in the morning.
You're the ones in the ruined party dresses,
standing out on the street, waiting
for taxis that never come.

the god of crushes and the crushed

Girls have to go somewhere dangerous every now and then
just so they know they can find their way home.

When he tells everyone you slept with him,
tell them the truth.
You were awake the whole time.

ROCKAWAY

fuck him.
get it over with.
you need a place to stay tonight.

you don't really smoke but you ask for a cigarette.
ask for another.
realize you're chain smoking
so you'll have something to do.
anything to keep from talking to this guy.

wonder why car lighters never work.
look for matches.
realize other people smoke
to keep their hands from shaking.
but yours are twitching hard.

focus hard on the radio.
listen to air supply sing "all out of love"
and smirk because it's so stupid.
realize your eyes are tearing
because it's so beautiful.
god, your nerves are shot.

remember how a friend said he hated blowjobs
because they made women subservient
you said he was crazy because a woman is never
more powerful than when she has
a man's jewels in her mouth.

wonder why they call them blow jobs.
blowing has nothing to do with it.

look at him and wish you weren't here.
realize this was a mistake and swallow hard.

touch his arm to comfort yourself.
see the track marks for the first time.
wish you hadn't fucked him.
wish you'd left the party when you said you would.
sex in cars always makes you feel tired.

drop the cigarette and realize
you smoked it down to the filter.
watch it hit the asphalt
and see it roll away.
keep watching
until the orange glow fades.

settle in against the vinyl
for a long night.

BREATH CONTROL

Who wouldn't want a good girl, a soft hand?
A gentle woman for a gentleman?

He said *it's been fine so far but after a while*
I want more than a soft style
I want some slashes
to go with those long eyelashes

And so the bedroom became the black room
but a year later he wanted something more
something I wasn't quite prepared for

He said *every woman has an itch*
and every nice girl secretly wants to switch

I like how the skins look on your white hands
I'd like you to deliver one of my demands
He said *every woman has an itch*
and every nice girl wants to switch

He led me in and lit the room with a hundred candles
and said *God never gives you more than you can handle*

I sat astride his chest
It's just a thrill he said
and he relaxed on the dark, dark bed
It's just breath control

He whispered *hold me here* and I did and his head fell back
He whispered *press harder* and I did and his eyes rolled back
It's just breath control
Just breath control

I saw him go pale
I saw him seize up
I felt something creep up
like a taste for this
Like a reward

A kind of love
A kind of lustmord

It was a minute then three then five then ten
he wasn't coming up again
I held on for twelve
I saw him seize and thrash and twist
and when he was still I lifted away my wrists
and looked at my hands and tried to understand

It's just a thrill I said
as he relaxed on the dark, dark bed
I sat aside his chest
It's just a thrill he said *just a thrill*
It's just breath control

When it was over I slipped off the skins
and drowned them in the river where we used to swim
and a year later in a shop I was stopped by a man

He said *I know you're looking for something that's hard to find*
and I think I have what you have in mind
And he led me to a glass case
and looked deep into my face

It's just breath control

BACKSTAGE

excerpt from "The Doll Killer"

> *"..bitch, you are meat you are something to grind*
> *bitch, you are meat you are something to grind..."*

the girl standing at the door told me how to do it. she said: you must get backstage, you must get past the border, you must know where to be. a list of people who can be useful: bodyguards, managers, drummers. a list · of people who will stand in your way: security guards, publicists, guitarists. a list of people who make no difference: writers, girlfriends, bassists.

once inside do not eat anything, you must be ready to talk. once inside stand or sit out of the way, but not in a corner, you must be ready. it is polite to accept drugs if they're offered but it doesn't mean you have to do them. put the pill in your purse and save it for later, you have work to do tonight.

you must be ready when it comes time for a photo, smile brightly, the rock star always wants to have a pretty girl in the photo for Billboard so it doesn't look like he hangs out with old men from the record company who look like dead fish. that would be bad for his image and this is a good time, it must always be a good time. there is always a party afterwards and you have to go. do not get left behind at the club, you will never catch up. do not get left behind, you will never catch up.

laugh at everything, everything is a joke. when they ask you what you do, lie. make it innocent, make it simple. you are a student, you are an actress, you are a shopgirl, you are not a spy. you are never a spy. you must get to the singer, it is status here, it is war. do not waste your time with the drummer once he gets you backstage. do not fuck your way through the rest of the band or you'll be doomed to stay on the b-list. start at the top or stay home. start at the top or stay home. don't worry about hurting the drummer's feelings, he's used to it. he will fuck some ugly stripper if he has to.

move in on the singer immediately. locate his gaze and intersect it. listen to everything he says even to his manager, you are collecting evidence but he will believe you think he's fascinating. all he craves is your attention. all he craves is your attention. this is important. he knows he's a fake but if you are impressed, if you tell him you've been dying to talk to him, that you are hot and bothered in his presence. he may believe you are The One, you are The Girl He's Been Looking For.

when this happens, you will know immediately by the look of hate in the other girls' eyes. that's when you know you've won. they will look you up and down sizing you up like animals do because here it's all about the alpha dog and this is just a bigger zoo.

sometimes he will want you to be wild,
sometimes he will want you to be tame.
he will barely seduce you, he will barely ask your name.
he will only spend a few hours with you,
two men outside the door will remove you when he's through.

so when he calls for you and says
bring me a girl that's already dead.
bring me a girl that's already dead.

lay back and say *I'm here, boss. I'm here on the bed.*
and know you are in deep water with only deep water ahead

and when you pray, your prayers are soft and dark and small and odd.
you whisper *bend me backwards and inform me of your concept of God.*

CHROME

So let's be done with this.

You said *I want you, I don't want another.*
I want a girl who knows how to suffer.
Chalk down my hands, I need to work the bars dry.

So now you're in the middle of someone terrible
and you're carrying a tiny crucible.
Every raw boy want relief.

You tough guys with the glass jaws.
Your bodyguards, your pins, your backstage laws.
Your French positions, your stripper damage.
It's more than you can hide, more than you can manage.

I'm done with the dark boys,
through with the dark boys,
done with the dark boys,
I swear you'll be the last one.

You dream of a girl with silver skin.
You dream of a girl cooled and thinned.
She's gone a bit blue around the edges.

You want a girl who sucks her thumb
when she comes.
You're just looking for a clean sleep.

She doesn't want to see you, she wants to be seen,
by the cameras, the crews and the soft machines.
You want a girl who could suck the chrome.

You're so rocked and wrapped in anguish,
some little tragedy I'm slow to extinguish.
Watching the suitors stagger home,
now I'm butcher, now you're bone.

I'm done with the dark boys,
through with the dark boys,
done with the black cotton mafia.

I'm done with the dark boys,
through with the dark boys,
done with the dark boys,
I swear you'll be the last one.

It's documented,
tequila scented.

You want a girl who's pale and bled.
You want a girl who's easily led.
Her slim hips, your tight grip,
tell me it doesn't hurt just a little bit, boy.

Come in, copy, she doesn't read you.
She fed the hand that bit her, she doesn't need you.
Your fill-in girls, your soft metal foxes,
your white receipts, your big black boxes.

Life doesn't mean telling lies,
it means enduring what you despise.

I'm done with the dark boys,
through with the dark boys,
done with the dark boys.

I swear I'll survive you all.

BELFAST

You lick her diamond and kiss her pearl
but you can't get the Belfast out of the girl.
This is how you throw her,
you think you know her.

Make up your mind as she makes up her face
she'll never really know her place.
You'll lay on her frame
and give her a new name
and bless her with all you can spare.
Empty as wire
violent as fire
you'll carve her out of thin air.

She's crashed home and cruised your world
but you can't get the Belfast out of the girl.
This is how you throw her,
you think you know her.

She hasn't left you yet but she will
by airplane ticket or kill-me pills.
Sewn into her dress, she can't refuse
(careful what you love, what you abuse).

She knows violence, she knows please
her hands for cuffing
and she says nothing
and hooks her hands behind her knees.

You fuck her flag and feel it unfurl
but you can't get the Belfast out of the girl.
This is how you throw her,
you think you know her.

Twist her arm 'til she cries uncle
crawling through your bedroom jungle.
Turn off the light, time to succeed,
she's China glass, there to bleed.
Her lovely throat, her lovely cough,
white eyes are smoking,
black sea is broken,
she's already destroyed, just finish her off.

Hold down her hand and see it curl
but you can't get the Belfast out of the girl.
This is how you throw her,
you think you know her.

YOU WILL

You will smile at me between courses at dinner.
You will stroke your ankle against mine when I'm discussing politics
    with the family.
You will lick away the last traces of dessert from your mouth
    and never take your eyes off me.
You will ask if I know what you're thinking and I will just breathe silently.
You will caress my wrists in the kitchen as I rinse the glasses
    in warm water.
You will stand behind me, your breath warm on my neck, my ears.
You will slip out when the others go into the living room for coffee
    and I will follow you.
You will clasp me in the yard underneath a tree, with fall air falling on us.
You will sweep in my trembles and brush in my heartbeat.
You will sniff hungrily at me and slide your hands under my sweater,
    blouse, bra to skin and me.
You will gather me in to you and your mouth will wet and bite me like fruit.
You will murmur and moan and pull me pull me pull me to you
    under the night sky.
You will shift me down to the cold grass and I will never once think
    that this is wrong, that I am your sister
    and you cannot have me this way.
You will not utter a word and when you are done you will lay beside me
    and wrap me in a deep blanket of stars.

IT IS IN THE LEAVING

it is in the leaving that the agony begins
— hope and skin stretched too far

time enough for words
borrowed and weighty

eyes that glisten in the knowing of what comes
always comes
after

airports
train stations
bus   stops
take us apart

but we keep knitting together
strangely inevitably
even we don't question it anymore

it is not in the reuniting that we are together

no kind of kiss binds us
each greeting
each meeting
is new is full of searching
of notsureifitwillbethesame

it is not in the continuing

not in the birthdays anniversaries new years
(although they're very grand)
nor in the letters calls poems

the *miss you*'s are careless because they are common

it is not in the waiting

the day-counting
the trip-planning
the bag-packing
no kind of agony that shreds days makes us together
(calendars are cruel)

it is in the leaving

in the last look
last touch
last kiss
one more
will I ever see you again
      rip
that makes me sure
that makes him sure
that this is a great love

it is in the leaving

A LOSS PUSHES ME TO HONE MY DEFENSE

there is nothing common in
your steps, your breath
so I let you bring me home
for some cool thrill
and let the CD
repeat repeat repeat
while you peel away at me

the air fairly reels
with your teaching me
to exhale and
cast off the heavy burden
of dead men

you take my face in your hands
and say *I believe you,*
just like those passed soldiers
who died twisted in threads
that cut them quietly
and made them bleed slowly

you listen to me say how
I wished they'd prayed
instead of watching television
and had chosen to waste their time
with me

there is nothing uncommon
in your words, your touch
just in how quickly you are
taken away from me

when it has passed
the memory of this moment
will keep me awake all night

BREAK

It will come on a cold street corner
after a lovely dinner,
the kind of evening that feels like
an American Express commercial,
where you are young and happy;
the kind that makes you feel
lucky to be alive and 24
with a man who thinks you are
beautiful and smart and funny
and worth his time and words.

It will be quick.

It will begin with him stopping you
and saying he needs to talk.
You'll gasp for breath
as you wonder what it is that you did.

It will hurt less if you say it fast,
you'll tell him.
But when he speaks it will be graceless,
ineloquent,
with sentences full of only dry words.

He will say it is him and not you.
He will say how sorry he is,
that you don't deserve this,
that he wishes this all came
at a different time in his life.

He will say that he wants to be friends.

He will finally notice how silent you are,
how much you are in pain.

Your hands will twitch
as you button your coat
against the cold.
You'll bite your lip hard
when the tears come.

The slush on the sidewalk will prevent you
from making a clean getaway.

US

There are so many of us in New York, you know.
We're the ones in bed early, with mud masks on our face
and dozens of unused candles around the room.

Hypnotized, we dive into potato chip bags
and keep eating until Ted Koppel's finished talking about
whatever he's talking about.

Birthdays aren't a big deal.
We try not to make a fuss because every year
we get closer to 30,
closer to not having, never having
the husband and baby
we swore we'd have by now.

We organize our closets,
make pesto,
hem skirts,
keep a journal
and read — a lot.
We have rented every goddamn movie at Blockbuster.

We walk by Baby Gap
and get a pain in our chest.

We start looking at our best friends and think,
hey, why not
— at least I know what she likes in bed.

We know how to make really good chili
but it always tastes funny when we eat it alone.

We sneeze and there is no one to bless us.

The hardest part is the music,
the songs that pour out of elevators and taxis,
with voices that crawl between our ears and say
This one's about you, babe.
This one's all about you.

ALMOST HIM

Excuse me, but...

I keep doing that. You know when you see someone who looks just like someone you know? You see them for an instant but the longer you look, the less they're there?

He's gone now.

In the dark with your head turned, you looked just like him for a moment. he was there in that glimpse.

He and I used to come dancing here sometimes, even though he was never really much of a dancer. I was sitting over there and I had to come all the way over here just to make sure you weren't him.

The strangest things conjure him up. We had this great big garden and I swear I can feel him next to me every time I smell a tomato on the vine. You know, when they still have some earth on them and they're warm from the sun and they're so heavy in your hand? That smell.

Or the smell of wet suede, or a cedar closet, or split pea soup. The taste of cookie dough on a wooden spoon or beaujolais, the first of the season. When it's still fresh and tastes so wet.

The feel of flannel sheets. We'd listen to I Love Lucy in bed with our eyes closed like it was an old radio show, and we'd be wrapped up in flannel sheets that were so warm and soft, we honestly believed that nothing bad could ever happen to us as long as we stayed in bed.

The sound of keys in the door. When my sister comes in from Chicago to stay with me for the weekend and I hear the locks turn, my heart turns over too. I mean, I know it's her, but until the door opens, there's still hope, you know?

It's like those old movies where the husband comes home after the war, or maybe he was missing, or he was in the hospital with amnesia and didn't know who he was, and one day he walks all the way home because he just has to see her. And she's been so depressed without him, maybe the house is falling apart or the bank's about to foreclose on the farm, and she's in the back yard, taking laundry off the line. When he sees her, she's turned away and she doesn't see him so he whistles some song quietly, like Moon River or I'll Be Seeing You and you see her look up slowly and everything stops, she's just filled with that one sound. And she turns to look over her shoulder, so scared it won't be him. Well, that's what it's like. Every time.

Memory is a funny thing. Makes you remember things that didn't really happen and forget things that did. I'm so scared I'll forget because if I forget all these things that happened then there will be no one on earth who remembers them. And if they're forgotten then it's like they never happened. No one can prove it. Some writer said people become our memories of them. So I guess if no one remembers you, then you weren't really here.

He used to say *I hope I die before you do, because I can't live without you.* And I'd always say *I hope I die before you do, because I can't imagine this world without you.*

He won.

We used to come dancing here sometimes. We never really danced, he'd just hold me in the dark. When you turn your head like that, you look just like him.

I know you and I don't know each other, but would you mind?

Just for a minute.
Just for a minute.

CAROLINE

the air is thin here
nothing moves.

your clothes are exhausted
your eyes closed.
you're too tired to argue about when it was
that phone calls became a quarter.

what happened to you, Caroline?
where was I when it happened?

at nightclubs you dance to the beat of the death rattle
and throw your head back screaming *isn't this great?*
you want to be magnificent, jazzed and wanted.
all you are is broken, filthy and lost.

you swim in the romance of laundry and cigarettes
weekly sex and notebooks.

futons are for sleeping
and reading and talking and drinking
and watching and staying
and staying.

stay on your floor
listen to the sink drip
and the cat cry.
tell him to shut up.
throw a shoe.

you will start a band.
you will start a magazine.
you will start a family.
you will finish nothing.

you're angry that no one's scared of you, Caroline.
they just feel sorry or distant.
you'd rather talk than move.

you sigh and say *everything worth doing has been done.*
when you think you're alone
I see you
licking the television screen
looking for your reflection.

hometown knows what you're doing
scared in the cave of someone else's car.
twenty is too young for this.
sometimes wishes get away from you.

strangled by furniture and checkbooks
you pare down
give books away.
say nothing when your drunken roommate
fondles you as you pretend to sleep.

after cutting coupons you hold on to the scissors too long.

you press your fingertips against the windowpane
when you're supposed to be out looking for a job.

miscarriage comes between moving and Christmas
and goes unspoken.
you spend the rest of the weekend inside
alphabetizing CD's and feeling unsafe.

eleven hours of silence for lack of something better to do.
your skin skims the surface of datebooks
pretty and unused.
just like you.

you have nothing to lose because you don't have anything
—anything you want, anyway.

when you give your number out to guys
you leave off the last digit.
you think they should have to work for you.

measuring days until the jackpot job arrives
now you're 26
have nothing to show for it.
you wait to be surprised.
you're still waiting.

(I am walking past your window, Caroline.
I am passing you by.)

you're hungry but you don't know what to eat
so now you just drink.

now you're west of where you were
—the part of your mind where memory and ambition
live, hang out and crash cars.

sometimes you press the button
on the police call box on the corner.
you say you just need somebody to talk to.

the last time we spoke, you turned to me and said
everything I love will leave
and closed your mouth as clean as a cat.

you throw parties for smart friends
hoping some of their hope rubs off on you.
you always end up in the kitchen crying.

friends offer kleenex and cigarettes
wishing you'll say you just want to be alone

that you'll be all right.
you always end up in the kitchen crying.

doesn't matter what it's about.
you always end up in the kitchen crying.

WHITE

I'm your oxygen girl
too pale to nail by the moonlight.
Too light to hide in dark rooms
too pale to leave turning in the sun.

Little lighthouse with winter beams
calling to pale painted ships
come in come in.
The eskimos have seventeen names for snow
and you still have no name for me.

I'm the smooth paper that looms large and cold
in front of you in your machine
waiting to be tattooed with your tiny tiny words.

Mine is an icicle tongue that stutters and wanders over you
like the dagger too smooth to feel.
Mine are moonbeam eyes that weave between night trees
to make wild things stir.

Baby powder cocaine sugar girl
brushed with dust and glory
of drift sky clouds and loose waterfall pearls.
Bone dancer with cool moon flesh lit from within.
Gamine girl slivered from soap.
Pale paper cotton sheet thing cut from a withering slip
too slight to hold too fragile to clutch in your rough hands.

Cool girl of ivory alabaster carved with mother of pearl knives.
Masking tape on a mouth missed obscene unseen
without color.
Newspapers rub off on my hands.

Like a deaf girl drunk on the feel
of her heartbeat
I am glass and water and silver
luminescent
a precious pearl not yours
never yours
on loan
never owned
not yours
never yours
no kind of wedding dress
birthday cake
fresh milk clean teeth color
but the watermark
the vanishing
the see-through pale flesh girl that grows and glows.

Enamel tap-tap
porcelain tap-tap
china tap-tap
crack.

Too light to hide in dark rooms.
Too pale to leave turning in the sun.

TWILIGHT

I'm the crazy girl you've been looking for. I'm the one on the phone that doesn't let you go. I'm the one who calls and cries. I am locked in a house of flames. The one who hears drums in her head. I lock you out and let you in. I let you in and lock you out. I'm waiting for them to find me. I'm waiting for the day when someone else calls the shots. My rape paper dress on fire. I've pushed this as far as it can go. My beauty comes from collision. Now it's out of my hands. I'm writing this in the dark so no one can see. I'm walking in circles trying to make a spiral to lift me up. I'm playing piano with a couple of ghosts they never say anything they just listen. I start with water I end with the moon. It's the same every day. In my dreams I can fit in the car. In my dreams the bricks talk back. In my dreams it's always twilight and I walk so slowly no one notices me move. In the morning it's over. At night it starts again. I fall slowly. I never get up. It's not a prison. It's a place. I like the buckle to cut into my skin. I count on the sweater to hold me up. I count the stars to stay awake. I let the food go bad. I let myself go bad too. I hang my hair on the clothesline to dry and step on the sand carefully so I don't kill anything below. I keep my cobwebs on tight. I'm wearing all my watches to listen to the time go by. It's easy you know. It helps you cry. Television never turns off. My fingertips are cold but my eyes are always too warm. I'm not getting sick. I'm staying there. I can climb a waterfall if no one's around. The paper always stays with me because the memory always goes. I could keep walking if there was a place worth going. Hungry from the lack of god, I read, curl up, cry. Do they let burnouts into heaven? Now I am blind and bitter and blackened. Have to pour water over me in the middle of the night. Have to baptise the other one here. This paper heart belongs to no one. Not even me. Sometimes I suck in the smoke just to spit it out. Tuesdays I'm an angel. Thursdays I'm a cat. Saturdays I wait for something to happen. Some day I'll break my back and pick out the bones like pins from a doll, put them in a box and crumble them with my hands. When the phone rings I talk to the dead, ask them for regrets. Sometimes I pray for someone to turn off the radio station in my head. Other times I try to tune it in so I can listen. Mostly it just goes shhhhh. I'm part wind, part dirt. I'm not what you expected. There are very small streets on my palms small enough to walk on. Small enough to get lost in. I would very much like to get lost. I've done the pill thing. I've done the misery thing. Now I'm knitting together the time. I swear I'll be there and I'll get there in a box. Maybe crawl out in the dark. Scratch scratch scratch. What I heard from the wind was secret. What no one told me was worth nothing. Brain turns like a bicycle and everything will have to wait. Stealing storms is no way to live. Next time I'll steal one for someone else. I'll remember to breathe. I'll stop keeping birds under the bed. I'll let the sun come up on its own. I cook my breath on iron. The door goes out the window. The sheets go down the drain. Everything wants to be free. Soft or loud. As sharp as a cloud. Everything wants to be measured. Weave what's left of the heirlooms into a crown. Storm around uncautioned. Have to have something sacred or I'll stay scared. Small pile of dust on the bed to lie in. Small piece of damage I can still make. Small war to fight in my head. Small ring to pretend I'm taken. I stalk hallways trying not to make noise. Now I'm married to the noise. Twitch until the heart attack takes over. Something has to. Have to get out of this head. I will write my dead name in water. I found religion in my wrists. It's there under the veins. I used to think I was a princess because my blood was blue. See?

HONEY HALF

(for C.B.)

You pass by those who would hold you up.
You piss vinegar into a paper cup
for the white dress women who talk you to death
when they wish they could talk you to life. Your breath,
your eyes, are of no interest. They want you to keep a notebook
of your progress, your thoughts. Later they'll want a look.
They want to know your weight, to know they kept you real.
They want to know what you ate. They say they know how you feel.

So you've found a way to fight the cold by becoming colder,
if you were younger you would hide it, if you were older
it would be hidden for you. All old maids eat like birds,
so what's your story, then? You tell it in words
weighed and counted like the Equal on your spoon.

Girls don't read those disorder books in their room
to derive strength or inspiration, but to learn
the tricks, the tools, the tactics on how to burn
away more beautifully. Anyone who believed that suicide was a sin
never felt the glory of deciding what came off, and what went in.

You can't divorce your family so you divorce your thighs.
You're startled they're shocked. It should be no surprise
that in a world of choices you have none to choose.
You're the girl with nothing, with everything to lose.

(I'll bring you back, you honey-half of a girl
I'll show you how to be part of this world.)

Normal girls take vitamins. I tried to teach you to bite off
        more than you could chew:
break off the sides of buildings, bite bits of babies' fingers,
        crumble pearls into

your mouth so their power would be your own. Eat the world and swallow
the chemicals, the newspapers, the feathers, the shells sucked out hollow.

Your hair still glitters from the party where you dined on water and crackers
and you entertained us all on why you thought cherry Lipsmackers
were nearly dessert for a dieting girl. We laughed 'til you fainted,
and we panicked in the car en route to the hospital. They painted
the room pink just for you. Now you say you want it black.
They knew to expect you. They knew you were coming back.

You tell me this program's for frauds, for dilettantes
who don't know what to be, or what they want.
It's not in the telling,
it's all in the killing.
To hell with these skinny-girl circle jerks, these therapy sessions.
Those bitches are showoffs, I'm so bored by the confessions
of amateurs, you mutter as they lead you down the ramp
to your room. *I'm real,* you smile. *I got kicked out of anorexia camp.*

(I wanted to bring you back, you honey-half of a girl.
I thought I could show you how to be part of this world.)

No man inside you, no doctor fingers in your throat.
You take full responsibility for this body's law and you vote
no entry. As simple as that. Now you'll be here
in your dead body. At least it's yours, at least that's clear.

These sisters of mercy in their long white dresses
decide who decides, decide who blesses
the carved-out girls, like scraped wood,
just slim and hard, anyone could
want salvation from quiet women
who whisper and whisper, thin in
their consequences, their prayers, their habits.

With your quick hands and your rabbit's
eyes, you cast off useless parts of a useless world,

and have found your cold hope here, curled
in the bottom of a dark dark cup of tea.
You never tell them your real weight. You tell it to me.

(I thought I could bring you back, you honey-half of a girl
I just wanted to show you how to be part of this world.)

No man wants me now, you grin to the fat white swans
as if these bachelorettes could understand, but they're too far gone.
Pills, fruit, soup, carrots, pills, milk, celery, pills, rice,
pills. Their whites are their bridal gowns. They married Christ.
Don't bother arguing with women who married the dead,
who circle you, closing in, coaxing you to take your meds.

Forget about getting married, you whisper. *I gave up in December.*
He made it easier when he started yelling, now it's so hard to remember
why it was important, and what it was for. I hold your hand and squeeze.
Standing up to leave, I notice the diet pills, pins, stolen security keys
in your pocket. *Don't bite off more than you can burn off,* you mutter
and you fake a smile, stating your manifesto as your pale hands flutter.

We'll live without it and have better lives without the suburban decisions
that unravel us slowly. That make the bruises. That make the incisions.
We will be sparkling single girls who dress well and are well read
we will remain glamorous city girls until we're soft and softly dead.

(I can't bring you back, you honey half of a girl.
You want no part of this world.)

THE AMBITIONS ARE

you don't trade money here
you trade information and skin

right now there are thousands of forgotten people
trying to remember you

children are killed because they write
an enemy's name backwards on the wall

young girls tie ribbons around their slender throats
trying to keep their heads on

chocolate boy walks to ice cream truck for vanilla cone
is shot dead
this city kills its young
maybe they've been alive too long

the angels all have guns now
the angels aren't anyone
you'd want to pray to

no one here has goals like get a job, get married, have kids
the ambitions are wake up, breathe, keep breathing
no desire to get rich, become famous, move out
the ambitions are wake up, breathe, keep breathing

every woman who walks by is every woman you'll never have
beautiful, quick and poisonous like mercury

this city is full of women, slim and busy
hoping there is room in some men's lives for them

women sort through the dead bodies like bags of laundry
with exhausted mama eye
sigh because they are too dry for tears

people huddle in kitchens clasp their hands
celebrating
something has tried to kill them and failed

nightclub men twitch
too subdued to recognize apocalypse
the ambitions are wake up, breathe, keep breathing
the ambitions are wake up, breathe, keep breathing

you have driven these streets a thousand times
and all they offer is their exhaustion
your nightmares have your name now
you exit the glitter storm, go home alone
and embrace the violence instead

this city has claimed all your blood and memory
this is cool and unusual punishment

you go for years without touching another
never think of the why
you are so casual about brutality

doctor says *take this it'll settle you down*
doctor says *take this it'll settle your system*
doctor says *take this and we'll settle the bill*
doctor says *take this and it'll settle the score*

somewhere upper east side parents
lock their children into whitewashed rooms
read the classics, discuss the bible
when children ask
whose life is this about, because it sure as hell ain't about mine
parents turn
embrace wall

the ambitions are wake up, breathe, keep breathing
the ambitions are wake up, breathe, keep breathing

there's a voice in the loudspeaker and she speaks your language
doesn't need to stay, can disappear when the wife walks in
here comes the interrogation room scene
today's the day you're gonna get caught

you're terrified of what you crave
don't get delighted they want you scared
someone is writing down your mistakes
someone is documenting your downfall

the sweet things don't stick around
but the bullshit lasts forever
please press pound

you're dual-channelling for new friends
or just new things to envy
who's running the machine you run on?

jazz bores you like math
now zero calls the shots
and rock stars chuck you under the chin

wish you had someone to speak code with
wish you had someone to steal things for
wish you had someone to fuck you so you could finally go to sleep
you just want to die a little bit

ink and paint is making you faint
in your pale pale shirts, stolen from uptown stores
watch the girls in the twin sweater sets make themselves
smoke, cough, throw up
teeth-scraped knuckles are a telltale sign

get in the car get in the car get in the car
and what you hear is the sound of impact
turn around slowly and check your body for bruises
there is no one here to take care of you

open-mouthed, waiting for a candy kiss
and all you get is rain communion
between lap dances and laptops
you seek girls who fuck like they're boneless

you're 38 and your job is telling 14 year old boys
what to think is cool
are you laughing? they are

and this one is a fire and that one is a flame
and this one is a spark and that one is a match
you put out in your mouth when no one was looking

and in your dreams your grandparents live forever
and you throw your love into the air like glitter
swallowing stars
spitting up stardust

the ambitions are wake up, breathe, keep breathing
the ambitions are wake up, breathe, keep breathing

mother wrings her hands and says *I'm so at a loss*
best friend says *I have come not to praise you,*
        but to destroy you with my bare fucking hands
the girl on the television says *you all work for me now*
boss says *come here, let me hit you just once*
man on the street says *I can make any woman kill herself in a year*

so you drive your dead body home at night
and when you sleep
the angels' kisses are mercury mercury
breaking love into lust
grinding pearls into dust

how old were you when you first lost control?
how old were you when you realized you could become invisible?
how old were you when you began to disappear?

YOU ARE NEVER READY

In four minutes you will be gone and I must tell you why.

When a star crashes, the angels are electrified.
Your life changes in ways you can't imagine.

When your dreams are perfect, they run like machines and leave you dizzy.

When you first discover you're dying, everyone seems to be saying goodbye.

When your dreams are perfect, they run like machines.

You must change your life. You are never ready.
You must change your life. You are never ready.

There are people you have to leave behind, they just dirty up your mouth.
They don't value your treasure.

You fall down, you kiss up, you love them, it's not enough.
They're nothing special and you're such a treasure.
If you had no magic here you'd be just like everyone else.
Imagine the tragedy.

You must change your life. You are never ready.
You must change your life. You are never ready.

Love is like crying like writing like dying.
You've got to do it alone.

I know it's tragic to be tender
I know it's dangerous to be kind
I know it's vicious to care.

Listen to me, I know what's going to happen.

You don't need a window, you need a fire escape,
you'll need a skylight to get where you have to go.
I can't tell you where.

And you dreamt that you were hollow
and you dreamt that you were whole.
Reconstruct what you remember
and it comes out in pieces.

You must change your life. You are never ready.
You must change your life. You are never ready.

Those below you can't hold you up
everyone is gone gone gone
everyone is gone gone gone
learn to swim alone learn to fly.

You must change your life. You are never ready.
You must change your life. You are never ready.

Cast them off like long rope and learn to swim the dark water alone.
Look up to the stars stars stars and know that this is your sky now.

    lift your arms and go
    step forward in Nureyev leap
    blink fast and whirr over streets
    hover over trees
    speed past taxis
    don't even bother to wave
    at the children who watch you
    awestruck
    brushing past skyscrapers
    and looking up up
    slip off the long skirt
    that slows you down
    and don't look back to watch it

billow to earth
tell the cool jets and Superman
that you're passing them
feel your hair stream back
with wind blinding you
forcing your dry mouth open
no one can touch you now
get out of this fucking world
as fast as you can.

DARK DAUGHTER

I am not of this family, I know that now
and I am not of your skin.
When you slit your wrists, you bled red.
When I slit mine, I bled mud.

You and your pills will search for me
search for my salvation,
will question the beginning of when I first fell
and offer explanations to explain me away.

The cloak of *the neighbors, the neighbors*
is all that causes you to quiet me.
No, you never ask about these brain movies.
No, you never talk me down from the balcony.

I count steps (sixteen from closet to bed)
and breaths taken in a day.
Cold numbers are warm comfort to me
as you can no longer comfort your dark daughter.

Every morning I am a new me and
select my persona from a deep closet.
I swoop down stairs
on fire, on stage.

Stop accusing me mother, I did not choose this.
No human hopes for a touch of mercury on the mind.
Some people don't go crazy.
Some of us were always there.

While you were having breakfast I was having visions
and I am slowly being rocked away from you.
Me, this baby that still wails away with no cause.
I am slowly being rocked away from you.

Four years ago, in the middle of dinner, I interrupted and said
Pardon Me, But I Can Feel Pain In The Ends Of My Hair.
You put down your fork then, you put down your fork
and fixed your attention on a girl grown wild
when you weren't looking.

Take away my hands, they weigh too much.
This body is not me, it's just where I live for a while.
I am more lucid when I give in
and I disintegrate regularly. The crazier I am the stronger I am.

Feel the cells shift.
Listen to the bones slide.
You hold me like a kite with a too long string.
Once I hit sky you'll let go.

I've begun my descent into self, into soul.
I've begun my descent and everything's fine
I've begun my descent and can't get off of the train.
I've begun my descent and you cannot come with me.

I look up to the showerhead, waiting for water.
Cold shock hits hard and slams night through
bones and skin and soul and brain and what was me.
Shudder and tremble and grasping the railing.

Damn your therapies
that leave me gasping
that turn me twice before I talk
leaving me with a long longing.

Self-help therapy helps no one.
Notebooks will not help me spew disease.
Medication cannot get me out of my head.
You cannot liberate me from this. I am this.
With a delicious shove I went over.

And you are lucky, mother, you are lucky.
I don't know the reason I am the way I am
so I wander round the house without a map
saying *I am not this, I am not that,* but I do not know what I am.

The doctors define me by saying what my problem is not
but throw up their hands when faced with a brain
beyond the radar, a gray lump more formidable
than their garden of books.

Give me some quality time with a trio of experts
tops in their field.
Don't hold me down, I'm not doing anything.
I'm just thinking.

I ask angels for prayers to string into a necklace and wear round my neck.
I lean against walls waiting for the day
when they open up and I fall in.
I am light with an awful lightness and drum my way through night.

I am not rid of this fungus, all the doctors will not cut it away.
No surgeon will open my brain and let the wrong leak out.
If they drill my skull the demons might escape
might take hold of their million dollar hands,
might hold on and bite down hard.

Don't you wish I was an abortion, mother?
Don't you churn at night and wish you had the choice again?
Don't you dream of laying a pillow on my face
and throwing me out with the trash in the morning?

I will rise up at midnight.
I will rise up and put on my wings to sweep over you.
I will rise up and hover in sky, in night.
I will rise up and forgive you your trespasses.

Use your hands and get me out of the straps.
Sign the forms and set me free.
Say you do not understand me, but you believe me, mother.
Release me from this white white white room unlike heaven.

Brain highways lead back to spine, back to the problem.
I'm crawling out of this wrecked car
but no one really wants to see me get up and walk away.
Trying to think takes up too much time.

The most the doctors hope for is to discover that my lunacy is new
is nameable with my last name, is discoverable for their medical books.
I might be an award, I might be an article, I might be a non-profit organization.
I might be noble but I am a loss to everyone involved.

If the bad side of you kills
and takes over the good side
is it a little murder?
Would anyone notice?

The neighbors say
We're so sorry to hear that
your daughter's brains
are dripping out her ears.

Am I crazy?
I am free with a horrifying freedom
and my world is full of flowers
and flame.

My typewriter scurries in the middle of the floor like a rat
and the bedsheets rise up, waves in a cold ocean.
Moonbeams are crystal bars that nail me to the bed
and cobwebs vibrate into scary nets for when I fall.

I am a thirty foot spire of unhuman girlstone
standing on top of the shoulders of unclaimed ghosts.
I am everything you fear
you will become.

Crash through queen glass and say I was right all along.
Rock this skeleton that has no use for blood or sense.
Throw stones at me so I can build a crazy house.
Stuff me with paper so I am full of nothing and therefore new.

I want to shave my head. Get closer to the shrine.
Find out why this globe at the top of my body
rules the rest of me so wrong.
I want to touch the disease. I want to know where I've been hit.

I have nothing to miss, no memories to wander over.
I rub my arms over the spackled walls and
wait for them to tip over
become floor, become sky.

You come up to my room
quietly, on the pretense of a lie
and touch the door
with scared, careful hands.

You want your heavy heart
to be relieved of 110 pounds
of bad choices
and bad memories.

This little problem is mine
I'll give it a name
I'll give it somewhere to stay
I'll take care of it.

I'll watch it grow up and take over
I'll take care of it now because I can
I guess that makes me my own little mother,
mother.

Don't try to open the door, mother, this poem is all mine.
Finally, something is mine and makes sense.
With a delicious shove, I go over again.
Big words reach up!

I swim over that wet line
and keep swimming.
I dig fingernails into stars
and feel my feet lightly brush planets.

Drummers thunder in my skull because there is no heartbeat
to confuse them. The thumps rock me against chair.
Color TV hums. Pillow shreds. Window releases.
Cat opens mouth, spits out bible.

I will come back in splinters
in blood in your hand.
I am looking through lightbulbs
and the storms keep coming.

The walls are crawling now, the candles are cracked.
I am listening for my breath in the paper.
Am clean, on fire.
Feels like water breaking.

All this is sleek and cut and fast.
I am to go free.
I am throwing up snow
I am spitting out keys.

This is a hate house
and you're breathing me in
you're breathing this sickness in.
Now I'm inside you again.

It's time to go and
all my   words   make   me   strong

Mother, I'm already gone.

GOD IS IN THE TYPEWRITER
(for Anne)

God is in the typewriter.

God stutters and bleeds through the pages
pushing my fingers to spin faster swim faster
through the milk and sweat
swim faster so I can get there
where they know me and know what to do with me
where I know what to do with myself.

God is in the typewriter
and calls to me with leaden prayer for clicking psalms
to chart my life.
All this time I've waited for a guide.
All this time I was writing poems I was writing my own map.

This is my church and bless everything born here
damn anyone who tries to enter
and God help me when I'm in here.

Holiest of holies
I write what I cannot say
I type what I dare not tell.
I wrap my lovely loves up so tight in the poems
they cannot tell it is them.
I shove my loves in together
and watch their eyes turn glassy at their favorite parts.
They can never tell what is the truth
years have taught them not to ask.
The answers shatter the fragile magic
the answers would break them.

So here I am, a pale witch with a luck for words
and a little radio tuned in to voices you cannot hear.

I corner myself at night and bleed by my own hand
under stars, under smoke
and write my way home.

(go away from your husband your children god is calling you
on your radio god is drawing you in on the tide go under)

Leave the dishes
the dog
the candles
the television.
This is all that is yours now.
This is all that will ever be.

Cast out your lines and reel them in
fish what you wish for
write what you will never be.
Cast your lines out and reel them in.

Little charmer, little stormer
write your way home.

ELEGY

They will not remember how you looked sleeping
or the words you wrote in high school yearbooks.
They will remember and measure you
by how you acted under pressure:
graceful and elegant
kicking and eloquent.

They will remember you for where you stood
and how you looked standing
with arms crossed
and pens full of blood.

They will not remember you for how many sisters you had
but for how many sisters you earned
how many women said *she speaks for me.*

They will remember you for all the things you disrupted
and all the times you said *this cannot stand.*

They will not remember the name of your child
but they'll recite the names of your books.
Work is only worthy if it endures
and while they'll never remember most of your words
they'll know the number of books born in your thirty years.

They will not remember what a terrible student you were
but even the professors you despised will say
they knew early on that you were
something unusual and fine.

They will not remember your Saturday nights
and how you curled up on endless couches
trying to create from your empty hours.
They will say you were a loner
and they will make it sound noble.

They will argue about how you preferred to write
with a fountain pen — or was it a pencil —
when they have no idea you slept
with six men in your life and only loved one.

They will not remember what you said
in taxis or at cocktail parties
but they will recite their rewritten versions in later years
proving they were smart to have such a smart friend.

They will not remember the time you were drunk
and punched the bartender at PJ Clarke's
but they'll tell their children that they were there
when you sat on the bar
and sang three verses of the Irish anthem in Gaelic
when your heritage was in question.

They will not remember you for a large circle of friends
but for the one who lived in the country
and adored you
even though she didn't understand you
or your work.

They will not remember the house you lived in
but they'll record the number of books on your shelf.
They will take it as a sign of your soul
and never notice how few were cracked open.

They will remember the shapes in the snow
when you and your daughter made angels in winter
and it looked like the angels fell out of the sky
and landed on your lawn.

They will swear you were brilliant
but cannot explain why.

They will complain about how
your translations and adaptations
are not true, not true to you
and that they are your keepers.
As if your spirit needed keeping now.

They will put your notebooks
on display under glass.
In your books, your books
they will look for you.
These things are important now
now that you're dead.

They will wonder about your inspirations.
The men in your life will claim
that your best works were about them
and you'll never be able to tell the truth now.
You wouldn't anyway.
Let them wonder, you'd say
as you'd chew on a finger.

They will finally publish
a complete collection of your work
— ten years after you're dead.
They'll include all of the awkward drafts,
all the lousy rewrites that said nothing.
They'll put together the brilliant and the banal
and call it art and put it on sale at Barnes & Noble
on your birthday.

They will decide your essays were unappreciated,
your criticisms ahead of their time.
That's why she died alone, they'll say.
She was difficult then.

They will never know how afraid you were
how terrified you were about your first book

and all the people it would hurt
when they read it and saw themselves
looking back from the pages.

They will never know how much of what
ignited your pages
was family fire or fantasy.
They will decide that New York was
a deciding factor
that London made no impressions
that Boston was of little consequence.

They will never know how you
apologized to each poem
before you edited it
as if you were scarring a child.

They will name a reading room for you at your college
which no one will read in.

They will appoint your daughter
as guardian of your flame.
Every few years she will publish
a 'collection' of discovered work
and never tell anyone it is actually her own.
How awful it will be for her to live behind your name.

They will never remember that for two years
you didn't write a thing.
Couldn't write a thing.

They will never know how sometimes
you'd wish you'd die early
so everyone would hurry up
and appreciate you.

They will never know how you
starved yourself in later years
because the hunger sharpened your mind
and made your words crisper.

They will never know of all the times you nearly surrendered
tried to think of what else you could possibly do
and looked around to see only books and paper
and laid your head on the desk to weep
because there was no door.

They will never know how many people
you brought into your life to inspire you.
When the affair would disintegrate
you'd say *Well, at least I got a poem out of it.*

They will remember you most of all
for that thing you wrote when you were eighteen.
The one that was in every anthology.
The one every college student was forced to memorize.
The one you tried to bury for the rest of your life.

They will remember you as common in life
but notable in death
and they will put a square brass plaque
on the ugly little place where you were born.

They will have discussions about you in lecture halls
and obnoxious professors will claim your intentions
to dumbstruck, unquestioning students
while you furiously thrash your wings
as angels often do.

They will remember you when you die
and far more people than you ever met
will say they were your friend.

THIS POEM

Please pay attention to this poem.
It will tell you everything about yourself.
It will inspire you.
Teach you, seduce you.

This poem will be mother and father to you.
It will wrap around you on cold midnights
and keep you company.

It is powerful, this poem,
and you will recite it,
screaming
against oncoming trains
You will remember it
because it is all about you.

You will quote this poem in high school yearbooks
because it makes you look intelligent,
slightly superior and distant.
People will ask you what it means
and you'll just grin with a Siamese eye and walk away.

This poem will hide one day
when you want to show it off
and you'll curse it.
It made you look foolish.
You'll find it later and punish it.

You will nurse this poem
giving it water and Tylenol
when it starts to fade.
You'll try to keep it alive.

You'll eat this poem.
First the nouns,
then the adjectives,
then the stringy words that don't taste good.
You'll gnaw the bones and grin.

SYLVIA

And you wonder how will you escape?
What pillow will you pick?
What pillow will you pick?

You've laid out mugs of milk and slices of bread
for your children to find when they wake.
A sip of milk and then... *Mother?*
The bread will be stale by then.

They'll be the first to see you there, dead in your yellow dress.
They'll look upon the scene and remember it
like a gruesome family photo they cannot put away.

One leg tucked under
your hands in your lap
head leaning to the right
resting on the inside of the oven door.

Every time they see a yellow dress — you.
Loaves of bread in the supermarket — you.
An oven door — you.

(Years of therapy will follow.)

The police will dust the house for fingerprints
question the neighbors
reconstruct your last days.
Put it together with Band-Aids and Scotch tape.
The theories will go on for years.

You haven't read all the books on your nightstand, you know.
You haven't left us all the words.
How does it feel to know that you're going to go — unfinished?

What are you afraid of?
That they'll find you in time
and the surviving will be more awful than the dying?

You're wondering whether or not to leave a note.
What kind of paper to use.
What kind of pen.
What to say.

These are words they'll never forget.
They'd better be good.
They'd better be your best.

As soon as you're gone, you'll rise
magnified.

You'll need some sort of ritual then, won't you?
Go on, count the eyelashes on your children as they sleep,
look at your bed and stroke your hands over cool sheets
that have never known a man.
Open your closet and nuzzle against all the dresses
from your slim-waisted days.

The only things you did right are in your desk.
Everything else is empty, gray, gone.

Funny how you put lipstick on.
Who will you kiss on the other side?

With all these last rites
you might never get around to it.

So pick a pillow.
Take the brown wool cushion off the couch,
the fluffy white one from your bed,
or the little pink square from your daughter's doll carriage?
(Don't be so cruel.)

So go on then.
Time to pick a pillow now.
Time to stuff towels under the chipped white kitchen door now.
Time to get comfortable now.
Time to turn the dial now.

>Time to consider not doing this.
>Time to get up off the floor.
>Time to pour a drink and watch your hands shake.
>Time to step back and see how close you were to going over.

Time to go.

BLACK BOX

If the black box is the only thing that
survives a plane crash then why don't
they make the whole plane out of it, I
asked. It's made of lead, you said, a
lead plane is too heavy to fly. And that
was that.

There are benefits to being a pilot's wife, you
know. You understand what torque is and why
San Francisco is always so cold for California. But
it makes you pray. Takes away your capacity for
disaster films. Makes you recite the oxygen mask
instructions like yoga chants (if traveling with a
small child, put your mask on first).

Parachute jumpers say that the more you jump, the more
your risk increases. You don't get any 'better' as a jumper,
your number simply comes up one day. The more you jump
the faster it comes. I thought about that every time you left
and kissed us all goodbye in the same order as if it was a
lucky charm: dog, daughter, wife.

When I was called on Sunday night, it didn't feel like I thought it would.
Didn't feel like being hit or having something drag heavily on me. It felt
like someone came to take my bones away and pulled them out one by
one. Impossible to stand, impossible to sit, I rolled and pitched uncontrol-
lably like a ship on death waves.

I was at the crash site when they recovered the black box.
I saw them put it in the truck. I saw them close the door.
I saw them walk away. I saw them talk to women in trench
coats with microphones. I saw them turn away from me.

The damn things are heavy. Well of
course they are. They're lead. You can
wrap it in a coat. You can carry it like a
baby. You can run to your car and drive
home panting, heart beating too loudly in
your ears to hear sirens as you disappear.

We   slept
with   love
now I sleep
with   lead.

I wrap my white arms around the
black box where you live now and
listen to you talk to me all night.

SNIPER

last Monday, they rushed out like
bright mahogany birds
to the yellow buses and home

he was claimed with a minimum of fuss

there was just a clean, brief ringing sound
and then the air evaporated from the school yard
leaving a circle of boys standing watch over the body

someone had set cross hairs on
a random black boy
ended a life and
scampered down a tree
to be folded into the city

they never tell you what's happened when they call
they just ask if someone can drive you to the hospital

that's when you know he's dead

I saw him in the hospital bed
his body married to tubes and wires
that couldn't save him
his face half-gone
the destroyed child I used to have

I pressed my hand against his chest
smearing myself with his blood
desperately searching for something
to keep, to keep

I shuddered and shook
cursing myself because
of all the things I told him
I never taught him that sometimes
death comes from the trees

CHILD

and the image of her unknown face
will shove back all the others
and make you drop your paring knife

someone will notice then
and ask if you're all right
you'll flash a quick smile
and carry on

at work
you'll stare
into random corners
absorbed
and you'll gaze too long
at baby name books
on your lunch hour

when a new mother walks by
with her baby
you'll clasp your hands
lest you snatch it and run home
begging forgiveness from a wailing child
that is not yours

IRIS

Iris is writing a poem while I read the paper at her apartment.
she blows a cigarette ash right into her shoe.
it doesn't seem to bother her.

I read the poem later and it doesn't make much sense.
then again, neither does she.
it's Sunday and I'm at her place again.

she plays Strauss and techno on the stereo
as people drop in on her all day long.
it's just that kind of place.
friends stop in and stay for dinner.
her roommate is dying but we don't talk about it.

she's the one who fixes me when I'm falling apart
— stitches me back together with nicotine and tea.

she's the kind of girl who can make a dress
out of a garbage bag.
she always somehow looks better than I ever will.
there's a lot of drag queen in her.

I lend her books and give her CD's.
we borrow pens and money from each other's bags.
we're beyond the permission phase.

she's not dating anyone now.
she gets crushes on guys and girls but nothing happens.

she travels to places I've only seen in magazines.
she's got friends with no last names.
you can't take a bad picture of her.
she falls out of bed and somehow looks glamorous.
I paint her toenails backstage before a show.
she's so pretty when she smiles.

we can finish each other's sentences.
she laughs a lot.
there's something wrong with her
but she won't say what it is.

she's the only friend who hasn't turned on me yet.
but she will.

they always do.

LIBERATION BARBIE

I'm visiting Barbie again today
but I get so upset seeing her like this
with all her bodies frozen forever
in clear cellophane coffins
like Eva Peron on display to the masses.

Barbie's dream houses are cardboard
and her surfboards, horses and Corvettes have a
shiny shiny hot pink shine.
God, she must be sick of pink.

When I was a kid, all she could do was
hang out at the beauty salon
eat at the ice cream parlor
or stand awkwardly on a fashion runway.
These days she's a rap singer, a doctor,
or a Naval petty officer.
But she smiles like a porno star
no matter what she's wearing.

Ken's molded hair and painted
bright white smile look painful.
At least he has a molded lump for a crotch,
Barbie only gets a weird dent between her legs.

Behind real glass, wearing real silk, are the real dolls
with really big price tags
($295 for a Collector's Edition of the Bob Mackie Barbie).
One young mother,
fending off an adrenalized munchkin says
That's stupid. You're just paying $290 for the dress y'know...
and I know she's never paid $295 for anything ever
no not ever.

Across from the pink wall are the Other Dolls,
not nearly as desirable, but they try.
90210 dolls, Shani dolls, Asian dolls, Happy To Be Me dolls
with small breasts, thick waists and short legs.
After closing time, Brenda Walsh and Barbie hang out
and trade clothes discussing late night sexual encounters
with Dylan and Ken.

Barbie's hair just gets bigger.
No doubt, millions of little girls in Mattel focus groups say
My favorite part is her hair.
Yes, I like playing with her hair the best…
So the hair keeps getting bigger
and curlier and blonder.

Pretty soon, you'll just buy boxes of Barbie hair
with no Barbie at all.

HOW MUCH

Math teachers try
to stump her
when they ask
her to figure
out how much
sand will fit
into a wood
box or how
much water could
fill a rubber
ball and she
can't figure it
out she just
can't figure out
the fucking math
but she knows
just how much
heroin it takes
to fill a
heart and how
much sugar a
piano can hold
how much blood
can fit in
a bathtub and
how much cum
it takes to
fill her mouth
and these aren't
things anyone wants
to know but
she knows them
and when the
math teacher gives
+ her an F

she just hugs
herself and remembers
just how much
her pale thin
arms can hold.

MOTHER WAITS

And mother waits
as only mother can
and speaks and listens
and tries to understand.

Her child is changed.
The ivy grown away from brick.
Daughter flocks home
for the warmth of a familiar hand
but still rages against its grasp.
Mother clutches her new rough pearl
and sighs and weighs the time.

Her child is changed.
There is a new tragedy.
Complex, unravelled at kitchen tables
strung out over tea and silences.
The air is deadened with regret
and cleared with consolations.
This has happened before.
It will happen again.

Tattooed hearts knit and fray
while they chatter the nervous, close talk
of sad women.
Dinner is navigated, breakfast ignored.
Collecting cups and counting eggs
they judge the distance between them.

Daughter sleeps late
while mother breathes black coffee
in the kitchen
twisting her nightgown in her hand
twisting her dreams in her head.

Daughter quietly becomes twelve again.
Her wrists are thin, her life is thinner.

They measure their words
as carefully as the vinaigrette.
This has happened before.
It will happen again.

And mother waits
as only mother can
and speaks and listens
and tries to understand.

The weeds are pulled
and books exchanged
the beachwalk conversation
drowned by ocean roar.
The days are thin.
The nights thinner.

They sort photographs and talk of the dead.
Curl blankets around them to watch the news.
Mother feels like they're sisters.
Daughter feels like they're friends.

The flowers need watering
the silver needs a shine.
Daughter is a magnet
drawn back to where she was last safe.
She touches the tablecloth like a talisman.
Tell me who I was. Tell me what I've become.

Asking hard questions over rough wine
tomorrow is long away
and night stretches ahead
as if there would never be a sun.

Their futures decided tonight
and their decisions weighing on their dreams.

Monday at the train
mother reaches out to touch her.
An object in motion will stay in motion
until someone breaks her heart.

And mother waits
as only mother can
and speaks and listens
and tries to understand.

GET YOUR HANDS OFF MY BROTHER
(for Bobby)

Get your hands off my brother.
I don't care if his name is Stephen or Daniel
or James or Billy or even if I don't know his name at all.
They are all my brothers and you have no right
no right at all, to attack any one of them.

What is it about love that makes you so scared and angry?
You fear what you don't understand
but how could a gay man earn such a beating?
You think you are mighty because
you are 18, ineloquent and full of rage
standing over a man with blood pouring from his nose.
Where in the world did you get the idea
that murdering a man will make your life any better?

These men are all my brothers because
they were the ones who came
to pick me up from a phone booth
after I got thrown out of a car.

They rubbed my shoulders in taxis when I was tired
and bought me a drink when I didn't have the money.
They went with me to Audrey Hepburn films
and taught me the meaning of words like 'fierce' and 'worthy.'
They made me understand that life should be about
things that are wonderful, things that are beautiful.

These are the men with whom I have the most in common
and they taught me more than Cosmo ever did.

They drank cup after cup of tea with me
when I was unraveling and reeling
from being dumped for no reason.

They taught me that love is love
and who should be the one to judge?

We used to say that if I was a gay man
or they were straight
that we would be lovers.
But in many ways,
they have been more loving to me
than the men I loved.

When my courage failed
they showed me the power
of a good Billie Holiday tune.
They told me to do what I believed in,
that a glass of wine can fix almost anything,
that the music you listen to
is the soundtrack to your life,
that $1.25 and a sense of style
will take you anywhere in this city.

They said *Everyone is a star*
and everyone shines
it just may be that yours
is a little different than mine.

They taught me that everyone wants
someone to come home to,
someone to look after,
that everyone adores a tender touch,
that everyone needs someone to hold them
and say *shh* when they cry,
that everyone likes to talk and laugh
and cook and watch TV and kiss.
They taught me that being a loving person
means sometimes getting your heart broken.

Whether by violence or virus
I've lost some of my guardian angels.

Patrick was killed in Boston
and I never had the chance to say thank you.
Lee died in New York
and I never had the chance to say goodbye.
Peter didn't want me to see him sick
so I didn't know until after he'd gone.
I hated him for that.
I loved him for that.

I made them promise they'd be at my wedding
and they made me promise that there would be
balloons at their funerals.
And I did because they taught me
how important promises are.

But it's not his time now
and I will not let you take him from me,
so get your hands off my brother.

(You have no right, no right in the world,
to drive through the city
breaking the wings off angels.)

He may be face down on the pavement but I'm not
and I will fight you to save his life
because every day
in so many ways
he saved mine.

CURSES

This is noise, this is curse, this is talk,
this is red, this is pale, this is ache,
this is last, this is slow, this is shock,
this is thrown, this is fire, this is break,
this is snow, this is witch, this is spell,
this is cut, this is final, this is fine,
this is moon, this is tide, this is hell,
this is hers, this is theirs, this is mine.

Feels like storms, feels like thunder
feels like storms, feels like I'm going under.
Here comes the slow going, here comes the pain
I fade out like a ghost, and run out like the rain.

All you know of heroines is what you read
sometimes we burn sometimes we bleed.
All you know of heroines is what you read
           burn   bleed.

There's a red red howling down my dark hall
I was everything you wanted, now I'm nothing at all.
There's a red red howling down my dark hall
I was everything you wanted, now I'm nothing at all.

All you know of heroines is what you read
sometimes we burn sometimes we bleed.
All you know of heroines is what you read
           burn   bleed.

Nail my knees together, this time it's not about you
you have no power here, you don't know what I need.
I'm giving in, I'll get there in a box.
Turn away, now let your legends bleed.

There's a red red howling down my dark hall
I was everything you wanted, now I'm nothing at all.

Drag a slow line down my leg
to my mouth from my thigh
show it to the police and the priests
so you can say that you tried.

There's a red red howling down my dark hall
I was everything you wanted, now I'm nothing at all.
There's a red red howling down my dark hall
I was everything you wanted, now I'm nothing at all.

I'm half alive, barely worth keeping
I rule the bed, soon I'll wake up sleeping.

Feels like storms, feels like thunder
feels like storms, feels like I'm going under.
Here comes the slow going, here comes the pain.
I fade out like a ghost, and run out like the rain.

This time it's different, this time it's close
this time it's between the spine and the skin
this time it's world wide and paper thin.

All you know of heroines is what you read
sometimes we burn sometimes we bleed.
All you know of heroines is what you read
                    burn   bleed.

HELICOPTERS

This is a city of the dead and dying
this is a city of the tired and trying.
You will die before your parents
you will inherit nothing
you will die before your parents.
Prepare.

There's a war outside the door
but you fasten hungry eyes to the television
to watch how others starve
the long skeletons that skulk avenues of mist and filth.

What does winter do to a woman?
It smothers the mouth
closes it with snow.

No one can save you now
no one knows how.
When stones scrape together
one always leaves a mark on the other.

Your mother's talking so she'll have something to do
there are too many dying, no one has time for you.
This city has you cracked in its jungle jaws
waiting to die.

When you sleep your dreams are stormy
you dream of helicopters.

You listen to your voice on the answering machine
it says *Help me God, I'm dying as fast as I can.*

Your heart beats like a metronome
you're only dead when you're unknown.

Your destiny holds you like a headache
write letters, cry, confess
someone is ripping out the pages of your diary
someone is destroying the evidence
you are disappearing.

Below you is then
above you is next.

Lie very still on the bed and feel yourself wither.

Dying is easy
you don't have to do a thing
you're dying right now
it's the fighting that causes friction
sit very still and go under
feel the skin fall away from bone
feel the shame of the body defenseless
feel hope hang itself.

Wrap yourself in a white bathrobe
and step out to the street and listen to the young girls
whisper about your beautiful pale skin
and how lovely and thin you are.

You are dying
they are dying to be you
you are dying
they are dying to be you.

Dismiss the nurses — this time you will die alone
pour out the pills into glass jars like pebbles and watch them.
Where is there to go?
Wait for them to come and take you.

Pour churchwax over your fingertips and beg God for help
in a language you can't speak.
Now is the time for you to moan in the dark.

Give in
let them have this body they want so much
the one they have to kill you for.
Let them have it.

Smoke more
it doesn't matter now
but keep the body clean
the evidence must be beautiful
the body must be beautiful
it must be beautiful when they come for you.

When the white nurses arrive dismiss them
you can disintegrate alone.

You have no time to waste
you have nothing but time.

Shiver in your sleep and dream of helicopters.

CASSANDRA

I am locked away
wrapped in the fillets of a priestess
wailing like the madwoman
waiting for a nation to tip its ear to me

blessed by Apollo
he could not rescind this wild gift
and so he spat in my mouth
when I turned away from him

(there began my descent)

I am only a thin woman with a nightmare
in my head and a choir of doom in my ears
and visions visions

my black eyes see too far
this mouth so far from mute
my faint breaths are poisoned by storms
too rough for this world's magic

I am all about destiny
I am all about fate
I am all about your future
and yet you turn away from me

in this cracked and tragic land
everywhere I stand is a sacred place
and shadowed

(you are all so enamored of violence)

such terrible pictures play
on the backs of my eyes

(do not turn away from me)

you call in prophets
and marvel in their little news
while I am underground
and no audience stands or sits
to hear me
and so I wrap the night around my shoulders

in my dreams you are all busy dying
you are so pale when you die

(let me save you)

my loves
you are all so devastating to look upon
when I trawl your eyes and see your graves
I hear your little spines about to crack
and know no Trojan hero shall live

it is so quiet in here
I can hear the blood of Troy
which will flood the streets

swimming in such a deep sea
I look up from this cellar
to see a starless room
and know with an awful knowing
of what will
what must come

I hear bells and horses
waves and wars
I see floors of blood
and I do not sleep
your deaths are swimming
over and over
in the oceans of my mouth

(do not disappear me)

there is no glory in this
no time for me to rise up
in robes and call for you people
you sad and doomed people
to behold

Troy
how do you sleep?

Clytemnestra
before you raise your hand to me
don't you wish to know
how you will fall
and who will take you down?

WHAT I WANT FOR CHRISTMAS
(AND OTHER HOLIDAYS WHERE WE SPEAK OF DEAD MEN)

I want to know how it will end.

I want to be sure of what it will cost.

I want to strangle the stars for all they promised me.

I want you to call me on your drug phone.

I want to keep you alive so there is always the possibility of murder later.

I want to be there when you learn the cost of desire.

I want you to understand that my malevolence is just a way to win.

I want the name of the ruiner.

I want matches in case I have to suddenly burn.

I want you to know that being kind is overrated.

I want to measure how much torture we can stand.

I want to know where your altruism went.

I want to watch you lose control.

I want to watch you lose.

I want to know exactly what it's going to take.

I want to see you insert yourself into glory.

I want your touches to scar me so I'll know where you've been.

I want you to watch when I go down in flames.

I want to crush the thing you love just so you know I can.

I want a list of atrocities done in your name.

I want to work both sides of the fence.

I want to have two cats so when one dies one will eat the other and
    nothing will be wasted.

I want to reach my hand into the dark and feel what reaches back.

I want you to turn tender when you have the time.

I want to remember when my nightmares were clearer.

I want to be there when your hot black rage rips wide open.

I want to find a way for you to survive all this.

I want to taste my own kind.

I want America to be socialized around creation instead of fear.

I want to meet your host virus.

I want to charm your sleep captain.

I want everyone to see the tiara break.

I want to be wrapped in cold wet sheets to see if it's different on this side.

I want you to play it to me over the phone.

I want you to make a scorching debut.

I want you to come on strong.

I want the television left on so I can sleep.

I want to crunch the numbers.

I want you to write your life story and leave me out of it.

I want to write my secret across your sky.

I want to keep you in the dark.

I want to leave you out in the cold.

I want to voice my concerns.

I want the exact same thing but different.

I want some soft drugs, some soft soft drugs.

I want to throw you.

I want to know if I'll ever be safe in the dark.

I want to decide who next year's dead rock stars will be.

I want you to know I know.

I want to speak hot metal fluently.

I want to know why you're starting to look like the last one.

I want just enough rope to hang you.

I want to hurt myself before you do, because I can do it better.

I want to coax the keys from your hand.

I want to throttle the bottle blonde because I know what she did.

I want to know if you read me.

I want to swing with my eyes shut and see what I hit.

I want to silver your hands.

I want to know just how much you hate me so I can predict what you'll do.

I want you to know the wounds are self-inflicted.

I want a controlling interest.

I want to be somewhere beautiful when I die.

I want to be your secret hater.

I want to stop destroying you but I can't.

I want and I want and I want and I will always be hungry.

INDICTMENT

All I want to know is whatever happened to experimenting with drugs sex religion food cars words school alcohol America whatever happened to saying the very thing you thought you could not say whatever happened to writing a letter you knew you shouldn't send and sending it anyway it doesn't matter whether or not you sign your name everyone knows who you are you can't even make crank calls anymore now that they have caller ID and no one buys candles anymore except Satanists and college girls trying to set the stage for romantic encounters and now they really can't talk to their mothers about sex because Mom doesn't know what a Reality condom is and she's kind of glad her daughter can't sleep around these days even though in the back of her mind she knows her baby girl might die every time she takes her clothes off but we don't have sex lives we have fax lives but we're we're too busy drinking coffee to think about that hell we're not even coffee achievers we're cappuccino achievers and those who yell loudest seldom vote and hepatitis is not cool heroin is not cool cancer is not cool it never was but thank god there is something that deadens our hunger keeps us skinny and makes our faces so gaunt that our eyes howl out to people on the street as if to say is it safe to go home now and where would we go half of us are living with our parents and the other half are trying to move back while saying how we're gonna drive cross country some day we don't live we just scratch on day to day with nothing but matchbooks and sarcasm in our pockets we build shrines to Lorena Bobbitt Maya Angelou and Anita Hill and all we're waiting for is something somewhere worth waiting for we shrug off labels and dismiss all of those consultants who sell our rap sheets and buying patterns to Madison Avenue all the better to sell us another chair at Ikea and we need something to kill the pain of all that nothing inside so we take Advil because it goes down like an M&M and we understand that we asked for a real future and what did we get clear beer but we fear that no one will ever understand us we fear that all we are right now is all we will ever be we fear that we don't know who the middle class is anymore we fear that pop culture is the only culture we're gonna have we open a Victoria's Secret catalog and think oh yeah I always lounge around on the porch wearing a garter belt we fear hope because hope means doing something

new our lifestyles have no life and no style we want to stop reading mag-
azines stop watching TV stop caring about Winona Ryder movies but we
are addicted to the things we hate and we can't stop going to brunch try-
ing to start a band defending Hillary we never finish reading books we
wonder why the girls behind the counter at MAC always look so mean
we're making lists of new ways to say cool we never listen to the radio
we never admit that America's best poem was written 40 years ago we
wonder why a woman still can't get into the Citadel we never go to
church but we want to be married in one someday if there is anyone left
to marry then and we owe so much money to Amex we're not broke we're
broken we're so poor we can't even pay attention we know that if we
were born to famous parents our lives would be different we would have
a show on MTV we'd be on tour we'd have licensing deals we'd be a con-
sulting editor at Details Steven Meisel would take our portrait but it's too
hard to work hard and since we weren't born into a famous family we'll
just look at the fishbowls and criticize it's something to do it's quite seri-
ous it's not funny it's your life this is your fucking life we're out to lunch
and we're gonna stay there our favorite childhood TV shows were made
into board games and we bought them for $7 at age nine sold them for $2
at yard sales at 17 and now we're buying them all back in chic downtown
stores for $20 at 25 so c'mon let's get stoned and play Scooby Doo and
you won't date anyone below your tax bracket you won't date anyone
who lives outside your borough you won't date anyone without a job so
you don't date anymore you hang out with guys girls gay straight friends
sometimes sexpals and you wish they were more flamboyant so you
could make allusions to Fellini or the Algonquin Round Table so you could
write about them so you could finally say you wrote a goddamned screen-
play so you could finally say you know what you want what do you want
you want to be famous and loved and happy you want to be in Vanity Fair
but you're terrified that you have nothing to offer this world nothing to say
and no way to say it nothing to say but you can say it in three languages
so you sell your lives over the phone to exhausted telemarketers and you
wear expensive underwear under cheap clothes and the chocolate in your
cup is not enough the Camel Lights in your pocket are not enough the
keys on your necklace are not enough and posting messages on America
Online is just the modern version of passing notes in class and you are

more than the sum of the Gap Beastie Boys Spin and Kurt Cobain we loved him to death Slacker was not a major motion picture classic inertia is not an occupation and Virgin Megastore ripped off a dead rock star and is running ads that say I hate myself and I want to buy our only participation in running Washington is Rock The Vote ask not what you can do for your country ask what your country did to you and you are alternately thrilled and desperate sky high and fucked Generation X isn't our name it wasn't even a very good book and Christian Slater isn't a spokesperson for anything he's just a bad actor with bad skin it is way past your dead time cigarettes make it easy to talk so let me make it easy for you these are the bad old days don't shit where you sleep don't fuck where you don't stay you keep playing you're played out so let's quit walking through Lollapalooza looking for fun a soulmate a reason to live a new $20 t-shirt let's pretend that a haircut will save us let's pretend that compassion is cool let's get rid of the X-girl t-shirts tattoos chain wallets roller blades baby barrettes and back packs let's pretend that we actually know how much money we made last year let's stop listening to white boys talk about all the crack babies they never saw the black girls they never met the drugs they never did what are you gonna write on your tax return under occupation cynical fucker quit whining that you haven't done anything wrong cause frankly you haven't done much of anything so let's talk about how we don't listen to Madonna's records but we really admire her gift for self-promotion let's complain about our butts let's get a membership at the gym let's never go to the gym let's talk about how we never go to the gym let's make dysfunctional families sound neat let's have another Rolling Rock let's get drunk let's stay drunk let's do drugs let's go into recovery let's talk about recovery let's recover from recovery Yoko Ono is so out she's in so Fluxus this motherfuckers all we want is a head rush all we want is to get out of our skin for a while we have nothing to lose because we don't have anything anything we want anyway we used to hate people now we just make fun of them it's more effective so let's stop arguing and start the car let's quit writing suicide notes on deposit slips let's stop procrastinating and write that book we've been carrying inside for 25 years let's admit that America gets the celebrities she deserves let's stop pretending that we understand jazz let's look at two beautiful people kissing and pretend that one of them is us let's stop saying don't quote me because if no one quotes you then you probably haven't said anything worth saying let's stop pretending that there isn't a difference between being alone and lonely let's stop pretending that this doesn't hurt let's stop praying for someone to save us and start saving ourselves let's stop this and start over let's go out let's keep going....

RIDE

Slow slow quick quick slow — ride.
Slow slow quick quick slow — ride.

At any moment, you know,
your manufactured cool could blow.
Welcome to the land of pointless and destructive.

You keep whining and crying into your beer,
complaining the reception doesn't come in clear.
You just can't make a connection.

What are all the pretty people on?
No one ever learns to speak American.
There are only so many Kung Fu movies you can watch.

Haircut, hometown, heroin friends.
You make excuses, you should make amends.
Who do you call for help when all your friends are dead?

Slow slow quick quick slow — ride.
Slow slow quick quick slow — ride.

Now they're calling to you from the bar,
and they're fucking with your film noir,
and you wear your hope like Christmas.

Now I don't know how to break this to you,
but her blue eyes were never blue.
So now the good times are gone, but really, they never arrived.

The terrycloth's beneath the tie
and another liar's caught in a lie.
I love you hangs in the air like a subtitle.

There's a war going on inside the bar,
she calls for the check, you call for the car,
and when you kiss her she tastes like hot candy.
Now you're just left to wonder
how she sized you up in three minutes or under.
She's out of your league, you're out of your mind.

Slow slow quick quick slow — ride.
Slow slow quick quick slow — ride.

You make an effort but she doesn't care,
she'd know that routine anywhere.
On your way home you keep driving over the rumble strip.

Things only feel true
when someone's abusing you.
You are sometimes startled you are never surprised.

There are only two speeds: fast and faster,
now you're lashed to mast and lashed to master.
Whether you're in bed or in court, everybody gets off.

Slow slow quick quick slow — ride.
Slow slow quick quick slow — ride.

So she smokes to keep from eating,
and you fuck her to keep from feeling,
and this is a taste
and this is a waste
and these are all of your days sacrificed.

You're rocking out in an empty room.
You've built your house, it's become your tomb.
Mmm thanks she says *I'll keep my options open.*

Now you're nervous with hope, nervous with fear,
she's barely gone, and you're barely here.
Here comes the cocaine wakeup call.

And like a boy, not a slave to fame,
you kissed lipstick only after money came.
Born in New York 30 years ago, you've died several times since.

Drive through tunnels and crawl through caves,
and suffer through a life no city can save.
They've got an unmarked car with your name on it.

Slow slow quick quick slow — ride.
Slow slow quick quick slow — ride.

Crashing down in a bathroom stall
coming home drunk and of course you crawl.
Next week you'll swallow your Corona in economy.

So she smoked to keep from eating,
and you fucked her to keep from feeling,
and that was a taste
and that was a waste
now these are all of your days magnified.

Style over content, you know the other.
Keep slugging it out in the superstructure.
If you love something, chances are you can't afford it.

Forget what's ahead and what's past
and live every day as if it were the last.
The dead man never knows he's dead.

METAL EYE

Secretly I'm dead inside

You know what you're doing
you know what this is about
you look in her metal eye
you kiss her platinum mouth.

Like frozen chrome
and mercury thigh
you kiss her mouth
as cold as a prize.

She's a dying machine
so bless her skin
and bless the nightmare
she's living in.

Open your mouth
all that comes is desire
she wants to die
with her eyelashes on fire.

She hides her star
and turns her ring around
she hides her wires
when she goes underground.

She knows what she's doing
she's almost done.
You think this is tragedy
she thinks this is fun.

Let me kiss you, let me bless you.
I'll bring my big secret to where you are.
I'll let you wear me out — be wild, be unreasonable.
You know I'm not like anyone else.
It's better than what you had before.
It's good enough for now.

What do you know about me?
You don't know a thing.
I know how to hypnotize you.
Don't tell anyone or I'll stop.

She's the girl
you don't understand
she's the girl
with the see-through hands.

When she was born
there must have been a spark
but there's nothing there now
in her cold chrome heart.

She watches you flourish
she listens to you fall
she sees you scrawl your love
in blood on the wall.

She bites the bullet
so watch it go off
and watch it explode
in her platinum mouth.

You know what you're doing
you know what this is about
you look in her metal eye
you kiss her platinum mouth.

Like frozen chrome
and mercury thigh
you kiss her mouth
as cold as a prize.

If this was your last night alive
what would you do to me?
This is a city where anything can happen.
One day it probably will.

Pay attention I'm only going say this once.
You'll survive all this and you'll survive me too.
Someone has to be in charge here.
Someone has to say stop.

Don't bother peeking
at what's under her dress
you should know by now
she gets by with less.

Your last night together
desire arrives like a terrorist.
When flesh meets metal
all that breaks is the fist.

When she was born
there must have been a spark
but there's nothing there now
in her cold chrome heart.

She bites the bullet
so watch it go off
watch it explode
in her platinum mouth.

At 3,200 degrees platinum liquefies.

VICTIM

I feel the motion of the car before I open my eyes.
The air is blue-black, brown-black, black-black.
Smell of gas, oil, animals.
I'm in the trunk.

My wrists and ankles tied.
My mouth is taped
and it almost covers my nose
but I can breathe barely.
I must have been here for hours,
everything's stiff and my head throbs
like someone's drumming on china.

The car stops.
He turns off the motor — there are no traffic sounds.
No people sounds. No wind.
What place has no wind?
I turn my head towards the sounds
like people watch radios when something terrible happens.

My palms are sweating. Where am I?
The trunk squeaks as he lifts it up and the sun blinds me.
He almost looks like a faceless Jesus surrounded by light.
He pulls me out of the trunk and bangs my head against the door.
I try to cry out, but it comes out like a hum.

He drags me, half-standing, along a dirt road into a house.
I can't see any other houses and it looks like a farm.
The screen door bangs behind me
and I feel a deep, deep pressure inside me.
All the rules have changed here.

I'm dragged down a hall like a bag and I look for a phone, other doors.
Nothing but bare floors and brown boxes in small rooms.

He pulls me into the bathroom
and I almost crack my head as he pushes me onto the floor.
Tilts his head to the side
and gazes at me as if I was a pet,
then walks out.

I'm lying there for a long time, trying to get the tape off of me.
My eyes are tearing. I don't make a sound.
I can't get up and I keep rolling from side to side,
trying not to make noise.

I've got to get him to talk to me.
If I can get this thing off my face I can talk to him.
I'll tell him my name.
Have you killed other women in here?

I'm thinking that you've got hundreds of them
nailed down, hung on walls, hanging from ceiling fans
and swinging dead in summer wind.

Why did you pick me?
If I had stayed to finish at the library
I would have been there 20 minutes longer
maybe I'd have been OK.
Would have rushed into the house,
books piled up in my arms like a baby,
and blurted explanations why I was sorry.
So sorry I'm late everyone.

Would you have waited for me anyway?
Would you have picked another woman?
Would I have read about her in the paper and said
Oh my god, I was there that night...
and called all my friends in a panic.
Telling them then how much I loved them
as if I'd never have the chance again.

I wonder what everyone is doing now. Putting up signs.
Showing my picture on the evening news. Calling old friends.
Maybe I'm not even considered missing yet.

The family will fall apart and my parents will go crazy. Slowly.
My brother will be so quiet at the funeral and insist the casket be closed.
(I never even told anyone what kind of funeral I wanted when I died.)

Maybe years from now they'll find my skeleton on the floor here
and they'll have to use dental records to identify me.
My family will say *At least we know now.*
We always hoped she was alive somewhere.
We just hope she's in peace.

When I sleep my dreams are crazy — I'm flying over fields.
I don't think I sleep for more than 20 minutes and when I wake up,
it feels like I'm under a heavy blanket. I'm still here.

As I wake up I hear a dog barking in the distance
and I think I'm in my parents' house in South Carolina.
When I open my eyes, there's a shotgun pressed between them.

I'll never get married.
I'll never have kids.
I'll never go to Europe.
I'll never learn to play piano.
I'll never write a book.

The last thing I hear is a click.

ALL WE HAVE

You grew sunflowers and swept up magnolia leaves on the patio. Left me notes on how long to roast the chicken. Made me a Batgirl costume for Halloween. Introduced me to Eloise and Bob Fosse. Took me on the Orient Express. Paid me a $5 allowance for the Sunday manicures and never said the polish slipped off when you did the dishes later. Stood by me when I decided to sue the Girl Scouts. Didn't get upset when I was suspended for drinking vodka on a school trip, and never told Dad. Said the other kids were shit when they made me cry.

Here's to the secret language of tomatoes.

Here's to your leather boots that I wore in the snow and nearly ruined.

Here's to the clippings we send each other, the same articles crossing each other in the mail, marked *Did you see this?*

You got the first phone calls. *Mom, they don't want me...Mom, he doesn't love me enough...Mom, I just don't know what to do...* I could hear your voice twist over the phone as mine gave out, shredding like paper, my throat burning. *Oh I wish I was there right now...* and we listened to each other breathe for a while. I still listen for your breath.

Here's to the last-Christmas-present tears that the rest of the family will never understand.

Here's to stealing the bathrobes from that hotel in Paris.

Here's to the keeper of stories.

On those brazen summer nights when my father stormed the house and shouted *You're just like your mother*, I always smiled with a secret glow. I have you in me. I always will. When I was dressed up for a party, he would softly say *You look just like your mother*, and I floated out the door in bliss, wearing your skin.

Here's to the jellybean hunts when you carried me in your arms because I was too small to find them on my own.

Here's to the notes you leave for us in the boxes of Christmas ornaments in case you aren't there for the next one.

Here's to the aprons, the recipes, the sugar.

I was too small to remember your mother's passing. At your father's funeral you wrapped a black lace scarf around your head and said quietly *I'm an orphan now* and I held you close. We slept with a knife under the pillow, afraid of the black cars that waited on the street outside, watching the house. We counted the shadows on the wall where the stolen photographs used to hang. We drove home with anything precious strapped to the roof and as you finally slept on my shoulder, the cord gave way and the wood box crashed behind us, spitting stamps like snow across the highway. We picked up your father's life in tears until the state police told us we had to stop, and led us away.

Here's to *I love you, I love you too, I love you three...*

Here's to the warm hands that lay down the dying.

I don't want to burden you, I just don't have anyone else to talk to. Last night was really bad. The doctor says it's between two weeks and a few months, but no longer than six. He cries a lot. I'm getting myself ready. I'm going through the photographs with him and writing everyone's

names on the back. I'm trying to be gentle but I've got to get everything
ready. He says he doesn't want a funeral, he says he wants a party. He
told me to leave him alone, that he's busy dying. I'm trying to be strong.

Here's to a late delivery. At nine months I could not leave you and stayed
inside for one more. I have never been far from you since.

You once told me you hoped you'd be the first to go, that you could not
bear to lose me. I thought I should go first, that I could not bear to lose you.
Now I understand it differently. If I die first, you will be without parents,
husband, child. If I die first, I know how cold your days will be, how long
the nights. I love you enough to let you go first. I love you enough to bear
the cold. I love you enough to be the last one. I love you enough to turn
out the light. I love you enough. I love you enough.

I send this poem to tell you of my love. I send it to you on paper. I send it
to you on air. It's all we have.

FIFTEEN, SHE LEARNS

That summer I grew two inches and stood
taller than the other girls. The neighborhood
boys who gave me no chance to speak
rated me as ugly, took me to the creek
in the dusk, so they couldn't see my face.
A hole is a hole, they'd say. I took the place
of the cold beauties who stood too far away
to touch or have. I would do today.

As they'd get off me they'd say *damn fine work*
and for a minute I'd forget a jerk is a jerk
and for a minute my heart wouldn't hurt.

As they disappeared and left me in the dirt
I'd wonder why I did this and what it was worth.
A girl grows used to the smell of the earth.

A teacher expresses her "concern" and calls me
"dear." If there's one thing to learn, it's who falls. Me
I Her She. I don't have a name, I'm a throwaway,
I'm a stat, I'm a report. There's a girl who plays
around in every school, I'm just this year's model.
They advise, they admonish, they punish, they coddle,
but nothing changes the depth of the rut once
you're in it. There are good girls. There are cunts.

She said they only want me for one thing, well,
at least they want me for something, I tell
her and the guidance counselors just talk and talk
and when they're done cutting me up I walk
back to class and say it's cool, pretend I'm fine.
Children are chickens and kill the weak. The whine
that pleads is met with a boot, cemented with blood.

I know the name of the brute, confuse him with God.

The slut always gets invited to the party last minute
like extra ice or beer. There's a game and she's in it.
How long before she's out and easy?
It's a blood sport, makes you queasy
to think of it now doesn't it?
But every girl wants to be a hit.
As I slide down the kitchen wall
they watch to see how fast I fall.

Drunk in the basement, I'm dizzy and fading,
in a room full of boys standing there, waiting,
and someone begs tension that needs relieving
(show me a boy that's worth believing).
Together we make a cocktail of surprise
with my soft ears, his hard eyes.

So stupid, I think this one's brilliant from the rest,
that he'll kiss my mouth before touching my breast,
but the light in the bathroom is fluorescent, a girl could
go blind from examination. A doctor would
prop her up and pry inside where she is private, shy,
but here he's not even a doctor he's just a guy
who came to conquer, who came deranged, who
knows tomorrow's not what we arranged. True,
I know they'll only steal what they crave and
how sad that no one chose me to save, and
that my worth was so low I was marked "give away"
instead of "yours tomorrow" or "his today."

No valentines, no heart attack, I
must get out of this intact. I
know everything I hold dear gets shredded
and kings become captives, beauties are beheaded.

They want to see how much I can stand
even when I'm lying down. My hand
is held down by one who won't speak to me in school
won't give away the secret, it's all too uncool
to confess that he liked my story,
my dress, my joke. So I'm a whore. He
knows he writes the history. Denial pours fast
as beer. I've no safety in a house that's glassed,
with windows soaped up by my little brother.

The vain girls who wreathe onto each other
can smell the cum on me, but never ask
Are you okay? or *Did you bring a flask?*

You learn what makes you cry so
you can avoid it. Inside you die so
like a soldier but what tight battle makes
you perfect, strong? Cattle takes
off across field. Girl takes off across sky
like a dandelion. What it costs, why
she goes, how long she's gone is
just a children's storybook song. Is
this a transformation, a survival, a way of flight?
How something ugly becomes something bright?

Reputations are like rocks you drag 'til you
bury them in a new town or they kill you.

At fifteen I had no choice and I found my
skill wasn't fucking, but flying to air from ground. I
practiced at night in the backyard
and when I fell on to the ground, hard,
I kissed the dirt and remembered the taste
of the basement, the creek, the disgrace.
Choose sky or dirt, I said, *choose sky or dirt.*
and the next time I rose, I flew, and nothing hurt.

All girls are born with wings.
They never tell you these things.

Abandoned the wood, the tree house, the creek, the slaughter,
the science book, the experiments. Your daughter
knows that a boy is a cheat is a fraud is a liar
and the girls she was taught to admire
don't hold up, disappear like dust.
The things we love we must
abandon like dolls,
keep clean the halls
that keep us clean. Girl,
this is a dark deep dream world.
Don't open your heart or open your thighs.
Your fathers are stones but your mothers are spies
who ask *Why is there dirt on the back of your head?*
but never *Did it hurt?* or *Do you wish you were dead?*

Boys are snips and snails
and puppy dog tails.
A girl is made of burnt honey, of sour fear
(tell me what it costs to disappear).

When you tell the story
tell them it was me. Me.

Neglected like laundry, she was a slip of a girl
who took pride in passing through the world
and leaving no footprints behind. Her
mother wouldn't miss her, wouldn't mind her
evaporation. (There are too many children already.)
I'll tell the next girl to keep her head straight, her sight steady.

You'll have to go in the daylight, a circle of enemies around,
like the boys who dragged you, the girls who knocked you down.
They'll all be watching you do your one trick, waiting to see
if it's real, if it's why you were picked, the girl to be

golden, the one to become a fairy when they became women.
You, the one to alight, the one to arise. Kim in
her denim jacket and pink dress, Rachel in her dark
coat and black shoes, you were selected in the park,
you were the one they'd choose, again and again. They
knew you were tougher, that you could play
back against whatever they threw at you and if
they gave you a lump of coal instead of a gift,
thank them for the unkindness that gave you this command,
that made their blindness something sweeter than
you ever thought it could be. It brought you
out from daydreams and bloody strings, caught you
between bible and bra strap into a territory you never knew would bring
a way to escape your old world with your new wings.

When I turned 15, I learned to fly,
and finally learned how not to die.

Also from AKASHIC BOOKS

Hell's Kitchen by Chris Niles
279 pages, trade paperback
ISBN: 1-888451-21-1
AKB19 - $15.95

"If the Olympics come to New York, apartment-hunting should be one of the events ... Niles's fast-paced *Hell's Kitchen* plays with the city's famed high rents and low vacancy rate to put a new spin on the serial-killer novel. Taking aim at contemporary romance, the media, the idle rich, and would-be writers, Niles has written a thriller that's hilarious social satire." —*Detroit Free Press*

Kamikaze Lust by Lauren Sanders
2000 Lambda Literary Award winner!
287 pages, trade paperback
ISBN: 1-888451-08-4
AKB05 - $14.95

"*Kamikaze Lust* puts a snappy spin on a traditional theme—young woman in search of herself—and stands it on its head. In a crackling, rapid-fire voice studded with deadpan one-liners and evocative descriptions, Rachel Silver takes us to such far-flung places as a pompous charity benefit, the set of an 'art porn' movie, her best friend's body, Las Vegas casinos, and the psyche of her own porn-star alter ego, Silver Ray, all knit together by the unspoken question: Who am I, anyway? And as Rachel tells it, asking the question is more fun than knowing for sure could ever be." —Kate Christensen, author of *In the Drink*

Synthetic Bi Products by Sparrow L. Patterson
341 pages, paperback
ISBN: 1-888451-18-1
AKB16 - $15.95

Sparrow L. Patterson's debut novel follows a nineteen-year-old bisexual girl on her whirlwind journey of sexual escapades, drug-induced hallucinations, shoplifting sprees, and other criminal behavior. Sexy and romantic, a fast-paced story of lust, deception, and heartache, *Synthetic Bi Products* is a compelling and original novel narrated in a bold, fresh, funny voice.

Adios Muchachos by Daniel Chavarría
2001 Edgar Award nominee!
245 pages, paperback
ISBN: 1-888451-16-5
AKB12 - $13.95

A selection in the Akashic Cuban Noir series. "... [A] zesty Cuban paella of a novel that's impossible to put down. This is a great read ..." —*Library Journal*

Heart of the Old Country by Tim McLoughlin
Selected for the Barnes & Noble Discover Great New Writers Program
216 pages, paperback
ISBN: 1-888451-15-7
AKB11 - $14.95

"Tim McLoughlin writes about South Brooklyn with a fidelity to people and place reminiscent of James T. Farrell's *Studs Lonigan* and George Orwell's *Down and Out in Paris and London* . . . No voice in this symphony of a novel is more impressive than that of Mr. McLoughlin, a young writer with a rare gift for realism and empathy." —Sidney Offit, author of *Memoir of the Bookie's Son*

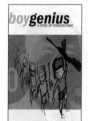

Boy Genius by Yongsoo Park
232 pages, paperback
ISBN: 1-888451-24-6
AKB21 - $14.95

A selection in the Akashic Urban Surreal series, *Boy Genius* is a powerful identity satire, the picaresque odyssey of a child seeking to avenge the wrongs perpetrated on his parents. Park renders his vision of late-20th-century global culture with the bold, surreal strokes of Pynchon and the wild political sensibilities of Godard; the painful, largely unmapped narrative territory of *Boy Genius* creates a gripping, harrowing read.

Jerusalem Calling by Joel Schalit
218 pages, paperback
ISBN: 1-888451-17-3
AKB20 - $14.95

"This remarkable collection of essays by an astute young writer covers a wide range of topics—the political ethic of punk, the nature of secular Jewish identity, the dangerous place, according to Schalit, that politicized Christianity plays in the U.S., and the legacy of the Cold War in the ability to imagine freedom. Schalit almost always hits his mark . . . This is the debut of a new and original thinker." —*Publishers Weekly* (starred review)

These books are available at local bookstores.
They can also be purchased with a credit card online through www.akashicbooks.com.

To order by mail, send a check or money order to:
Akashic Books
PO Box 1456
New York, NY 10009

Prices include shipping. Outside the U.S., add $3 to each book ordered.

Nicole Blackman's work has appeared in numerous major anthologies including *Aloud: Voices from the Nuyorican Poets Cafe, Verses That Hurt,* and *Poetry Nation.* Blackman has performed on over fifteen albums, including recordings with Golden Palominos, KMFDM, Recoil, Bill Laswell, and Scanner. She performs internationally and lives in New York.